SOUTHDOWN BUSES IN PRESERVATION

SIMON STANFORD

AMBERLEY

First published 2024

Amberley Publishing
The Hill, Stroud
Gloucestershire, GL5 4EP

www.amberley-books.com

ISBN 978 1 3981 1937 6 (print)
ISBN 978 1 3981 1938 3 (ebook)

British Library Cataloguing in Publication Data.
A catalogue record for this book is available from the British Library.

Origination by Amberley Publishing.
Printed in the UK.

Introduction

Southdown Motor Services was formed in 1915 and became very well known for the green and cream colours with gold fleet names on their buses and coaches, which would be seen all over Sussex and parts of Hampshire. National Bus Company ownership in 1969 and Stagecoach ownership twenty years later saw the traditional colour scheme diminish, although Southdown revived the traditional livery and repainted some coaches two-tone green in the 1980s.

Many books have been written about Southdown, an enthusiasts' club exists, models are made of Southdown buses and coaches, and collectors collect just about anything connected with this famous company. Despite the fact Southdown was taken over by Stagecoach over thirty years ago, memorabilia changes hands online and at rally stalls for significant amounts of money. The Southdown vehicle preservation list has seen some vehicles disappear from the rally scene recently, which could be down to financial reasons. The cost of living crisis will have had an impact on hobbies, coupled with lack of suitable storage facilities, and their cost.

Remarkably, there remains over a hundred Southdown buses and coaches in preservation at the time of writing. Some have been lovingly restored to their original condition, achieving a high standard, whilst some are preserved but awaiting restoration in storage, and regrettably some languish in poor condition due to lack of funds. A handful of these buses are licensed to carry fare-paying passengers and earn their keep on hire to transport passengers back in time.

Southdown green and cream lives on, and preserved buses and coaches are a familiar sight at bus rallies and shows during the season. Some buses are over a century old. In addition, memorabilia and other artifacts – bus stops, bus garages, ticket machines, timetables, uniforms and other ephemera – are preserved too; private collectors like me store most of it in spare rooms or attics. Museums also display these items for us to enjoy Southdown's history.

The book looks at Southdown in preservation with photos and captions of buses and coaches fortunate to be in the hands of dedicated people; without them the past can easily be forgotten. Some buses that have not been so fortunate as to end up in preservation are included in this pictorial history, as are one or two from the operating area of Southdown such as the Brighton Hove and District and Eastbourne Corporation.

A close-up image of the iconic Southdown scroll, as fitted to the front of all buses and coaches in the era of Southdown's traditional livery. This badge is fitted to a preserved coach.

FUF 181 is a 1939 Dennis Falcon with coachwork by Harrington of Hove in Sussex. Delivered to Southdown just after the outbreak of the Second World War for the Worthing Tramocar services, and one of the earliest examples of Southdown single-deck buses in preservation. (Photographed by Michael Taylor at Ardingly, Sussex, June 1970)

Another Ardingly view of FUF 181 in 1970. It had an active start in its preserved life, attending many rallies and the London to Brighton Commercial Vehicle Run on several occasions. I should imagine this Dennis was a product of the factory in Guildford, Surrey, sadly no longer in existence. The Harrington factory that built the bodywork closed in 1966. (Thanks to Michael Taylor)

A rear view of Dennis Falcon FUF 181 in 1970 – note the period advertising. After an active life attending shows and rallies, it was withdrawn from the rally scene in the early 1970s and stored in various locations. I understand it still survives, some eighty-four years after being built. (Thanks to Michael Taylor)

This offside rear view completes four all-round views of this Dennis Falcon with Harrington bodywork, new in 1939. (My thanks to Michael Taylor, who photographed FUF 181 at Ardingly in Sussex. Michael lives in Canada and kindly allowed me use of his photographs)

AUF 666, a Leyland TD3 new to Southdown in 1934 and receiving a new body by Beadle in 1949. A resident on the Isle of Wight when this photo was taken, it was secured for preservation in the 1970s and clearly demonstrates the amount of restoration work required.

UF 1517 is a 1927 Dennis with a nineteen-seat, all-aluminium body by Short Brothers. It became a garden chalet during its life after disposal by Southdown. Now fully restored and part of the collection kept at Amberley Museum where the photo was taken, it has ventured out many times to take part in events in Worthing and Southsea. (April 2023)

The roaring '20s, as that decade is known, are represented in this black-and-white photo of UF 4813, a 1929 Leyland TD1, and CD 7045, a Leyland G7 new in 1922. They are on display together at Southsea at a popular bus rally with preserved Southdown buses.

Back to the 1920s, this time in colour, and on display at Southsea again are UF 4813 and CD 7045. Study the photo to see the attention to detail in the restoration and preservation – from the apple green and primrose paintwork to the period advertising.

On display at the Amberley Museum spring bus show in April 2023, no doubt resting in between trips around the museum ground, is UF 4813, a 1929 Leyland TD1 looking resplendent and well cared for in preservation having joined other vehicles in the Southdown Omnibus Trust vehicles collection.

One of the benefits of the preserved former Southdown buses being stored at Amberley are the bus rides around the museum site. At the spring bus show in April 2023, UF 4813 passes the period street furniture, which adds detail to the preservation of the Southdown bus scene.

A rear view of UF 4813 in April 2023. The open-top and open-staircase design of this period was built by Brush in Leicestershire. This is a unique survivor of this type. A regular attendee of events around the south-east, 813 has recently been acquired by the Southdown Omnibus Trust, joining other former Southdown buses at Amberley Museum.

A black-and-white view of UF 4813 on one of its many outings arriving on Maderia Drive, Brighton, having completed the London to Brighton Commercial Vehicle Run in May 1985. No stranger to Brighton in its operating days with Southdown, it would have worked open-top services in the area.

A pair of single-deckers from the 1930s. Fleet number 1205 (UF 6805) is a 1930 Tilling Stevens with thirty-one-seat bodywork by Short Brothers. Fleet number 24 (ECD 524) is a 1937 Leyland Cub with bodywork by Park Royal and seats twenty. Both buses are kept at Amberley. This photo was taken at the spring bus show in April 2023.

A rear view of 1205 (UF 6805) and 24 (ECD 524) taken at Amberley Museum in 2023. The quality of the initial restoration and continued preservation of these two is amazing. Clearly visible on 1205 is the ladder to access the roof-mounted luggage rack.

UF 6805, the 1930 Tilling Stevens photographed at Amberley Museum, has an interesting history. Having been requisitioned by the War Department in 1940, it has been used to transport prisoners of war and has even been a chicken shed. Extensive restoration has returned this bus to its former glory. A credit to those involved in the rebuild.

New in 1914 and a survivor of two world wars is IB 552, a Tilling Stevens TS3 with a Newman forty-seat body. It carries the Worthing Motor Services name, a precursor to Southdown. Although a resident at Amberley Museum, it is out for the day to take part in the 2004 Worthing bus rally.

ECD 524, a 1937 Leyland Cub, awaits passengers at the Amberley Museum spring bus show in 2023. It is a popular bi-annual event where one can ride on preserved Southdown buses around the museum grounds. There aren't too many opportunities to enjoy a ride on an eighty-six-year-old bus in such beautiful surroundings.

ECD 524 giving rides to pleasure-seeking passengers around the Amberley Museum grounds. No. 24 in the Southdown fleet, it was purchased for preservation in 1969. Acquired by the Southdown Omnibus Trust *c.* 2002, it was completely restored in time for the Amberley bus show in 2013.

A rear view of ECD 524. Its twenty-seat Park Royal bodywork is looking superb at Amberley Museum in 2023, no doubt awaiting its next trip to take passengers around the museum grounds. The extensive restoration was carried out in one of the former Southdown garages at the museum.

ECD 524 is on display at the Worthing bus rally in July 2023. In addition to the preservation of this beautifully restored Leyland Cub, note the boards offering excursions to Arundel Castle and Long Furlong, preserving the era of Southdown.

ECD 524 on Worthing seafront in July 2023. After withdrawal by Southdown *c.* 1954 it was used by a theatre company until purchased for preservation. Restoration included the detailed destination displays. Villages in rural areas were served by the Southdown bus services in Sussex and Hampshire.

CCD 940 is a 1936 Leyland Titan TD4 with Beadle bodywork and received a new body by East Lancs Coachbuilders in 1950. This 1992 photo shows it at the Bournemouth Corporation depot. Preserved but not restored, it has had several owners in recent years around the country but is believed to be back in Sussex awaiting restoration.

A return to the 1920s with CD 5125, a Leyland N type with Short Brothers open-top, open-staircase bodywork, which it received in 1928. Restored and preserved, it is seen at Amberley in April 2023 preparing to take passengers around the museum grounds.

A black-and-white picture of Leyland N type CD 5125 at Battersea in 1979 taking part in the London to Brighton Commercial Run. New with solid tyres but converted to run on pneumatic tyres, this delightful bus is owned by the Southdown Omnibus Trust and is an Amberley resident.

Staying with the 1920s is CD 7045, which was new to Southdown in 1922. Carrying on the Leyland theme, this one is a G7 with Short Brothers bodywork. Preserved for many years by Southdown, it passed to Stagecoach when they purchased the company in 1989. It is now part of the Scottish Vintage Bus Museum's collection in Lathalmond. (Photo taken in 2003)

The second Leyland Cub to feature amongst these preserved vehicles once owned by Southdown is CUF 404, which was new in 1936 with bodywork by Harrington. After withdrawal in *c.* 1953, it continued its passenger-carrying career in Jersey for around ten years, returning to the mainland for preservation.

From 1937 is DUF 179, a Leyland Tiger TS7 with coachwork by Harrington of Hove, pictured here at Amberley Museum grounds. From *c.* 2012 it joined the preserved bus collection of Ensignbus in Essex, undergoing a full restoration.

Leyland Tiger TS7 DUF 179 on display at one of the many bus rallies that take place during the summer months. London to Brighton express services were part of frequently run excursions using this type of bus. It is one of many vehicles to feature in this book that survived the Second World War.

To the 1940s now with GUF 727, a 1947 Leyland Tiger PS1 with bodywork by ECW of Lowestoft. Used on express services with Southdown, it later served as a 'left luggage' office at Bognor. It has now been restored and preserved. This photo was taken in Worthing in 2002.

A Leyland PS1 with ECW bodywork, HCD 449 from 1947 is one of twenty-five built for long-distance express services. It was the second to serve as a 'left luggage' office in Bognor. Restored and preserved, it is photographed at Amberley Museum giving rides to visitors.

An advantage to riding around Amberley Museum at the bus shows is the opportunity to take photos from an open-top bus and get some unique shots, like this close-up view of Leyland PS1 HCD 449 on display outside one of the Southdown garages.

Photographed at Buxted railway station taking part in a vintage bus day is PUF 647, a 1956 Guy Arab with Park Royal body. The only known survivor of forty-eight Guys delivered to Southdown in 1955 and 1956.

Guy Arab PUF 647 has returned home after a service and MOT carried out by your author. I had just driven it some 60 miles from the workshop to its home via the testing station. Some might say it's hard work, but it was a most enjoyable experience driving through the Sussex countryside.

In the early days of its preservation Guy Arab PUF 647, new in 1956, leads a cavalcade of buses to celebrate the Southampton transport centenary in 1979. Number 547 in the Southdown fleet has become a familiar sight at various shows and rallies.

It is 1996 and PUF 647 is taking part in the Worthing bus rally and running day. This is a rally I have attended many times, where preserved buses run various routes, some long-since discontinued. A good opportunity to ride on preserved Southdown buses.

AUF 670, a 1934 Leyland Titan TD3, was originally bodied by Short Brothers then was rebodied by East Lancs Coachbuilders in 1946. It is seen here beautifully restored and just arriving at the 1992 Southsea bus rally. Destination displays are an important part of bus restoration and these are showing Portsmouth area destinations.

AUF 670 is a well-travelled bus, having had homes at various locations around the country. It is photographed in 2021 in Taunton, Somerset, taking part in a bus running day. I believe it has settled with a preservationist on the south coast. (Thanks to Steve Cockram for use of the photo)

AUF 670 was fleet number 970 with Southdown when new in 1934. After surviving the Second World War it received a new body in 1946. Previous use for this bus was a timing point control at Badminton Horse Trials in Gloucestershire.

New in 1955, OCD 772 is a Leyland PD2 with bodywork by Park Royal. A former driver training bus with Southdown, it was acquired for preservation in yellow training bus colours. (Photographed at Cobham bus rally in 1984)

OCD 772 repainted in Southdown green and cream. When buses were acquired directly from Southdown the condition was normally very good, meaning restoration was not such a daunting task. 772 was purchased from Southdown *c.* 1982.

Another Leyland Titan PD2 to be preserved was JCD 81, dating from 1948. After disposal by Southdown it was purchased for preservation *c.* 1968 in the north of England. It returned south to Brighton in 1974. After being vandalised it was sadly scrapped in 1976.

From 1948 is Leyland Tiger PS1 with thirty-two-seat bodywork by Park Royal. After disposal by Southdown, it spent a lot of time in the north of England and found a preservation home in the Stockport area. (Picture from an acquired slide collection)

Parked on Maderia Drive in Brighton is GCD 48. It dates from 1939, new when the Second World War was imminent. A Leyland TD5 rebodied in 1950 by Park Royal. Picture from an acquired slide collection.

GCD 48 is seen on display at the 2010 Worthing bus rally. The 1939 Leyland TD5 looks resplendent after a thorough restoration, a remarkable survivor of the Second World War and wonderful to see in attendance at rallies and shows.

In attendance at the Cobham bus rally is 1953 Leyland MUF 488, a Beadle of Kent built integral with running units from Leyland. Integral buses became common from the 1970s but were quite rare in the 1950s.

MUF 650 started life with Southdown in 1953 as s Duple-bodied Leyland Royal Tiger coach. After withdrawal in 1966 and a short time with a construction company for staff transport, the body was removed and the chassis exported to Malta. A new body was fitted *c.* 1973 and entered service in Malta for some thirty years, returning to England in 2013 for preservation. Photographed at Southsea in 2015.

A frontal shot of MUF 650 in June 2015. After various Maltese registration plates, it now carries its original number plate once again. It is truly remarkable how this Leyland Royal Tiger chassis has survived some sixty-two years; perhaps the Maltese climate has something to do with it.

Two preserved Leylands together. RUF 205 is from 1957 with a PD2 body by East Lancs. GCD 48 is from 1939 with a TD5 body by Park Royal. Southdown was a loyal Leyland customer and it is pleasing to see so many of them preserved and restored to a high standard.

RUF 205 at Southsea in 1992, around a year after acquisition for preservation. Fleet number 805 with Southdown, it dates from 1957 and has bodywork by East Lancs of Blackburn, a bus bodybuilder that sadly closed in 2012.

RUF 205 was withdrawn by Southdown in 1971 and saw further use in Essex and in Cambridgeshire with the well-respected Kenzie's of Shepreth. Preservation possibilities have often languished in yards for many years, making the restoration unviable, but this was not the case here.

Old Portsmouth in the 1990s is the location of Leyland PD2 RUF 205. The picture is from a collection of slides I acquired. At the time of writing it is having further restoration work carried out, thus securing an even longer future.

Leyland PD2 786 (RUF 186) and Leyland PD3 260 (BUF 260C) are at Amberley, and this is not the first time they have been photographed together. Both buses have had an active life since withdrawal by Southdown and before preservation, with 260 seeing use in Cambridgeshire and 786 in France.

Cobham's 2009 bus show and on display is 1956 Beadle-bodied Leyland PD2 RUF 186, one of two from this batch new in 1956/57. It is looking very well presented – note the neat destination display.

Six years after the previous photo, in September 2015, RUF 186 is now taking part in the Amberley autumn bus show, giving rides to visitors around the site. A notable difference in this view is the repositioning of the number plate to below the driver's windscreen.

Leyland Tiger Cub with coachwork by Weymann. XUF 141, fleet number 1141 with Southdown, was new to the company in March 1960, a luxury touring coach of that period with thirty-seven seats that no doubt would have visited much of the UK throughout its career. Seen here at Cobham bus show in 2009.

XUF 141 at Southsea bus show in 1996. Immaculately restored and preserved since the early 1990s, this is a joy to see in attendance at many shows and rallies. Oxford Diecast made a fine model of the Leyland Tiger Cub *c.* 2014 which proves popular amongst collectors.

Formerly a Leyland TD5 double-deck bus with Beadle bodywork, EUF 184 was converted to a tow wagon *c.* 1957. It finally got to retire in the mid-1980s and now lives at Amberley Museum where this photo was taken in 2023.

An impressive line-up of five preserved Southdown buses – three Leylands, a Guy and a Bristol, all looking very well presented. The oldest bus in this view is UF 7428, which is seen elsewhere in this book, and Bristol UUF 110J is the newest. There is an incredible forty years between the two.

A trio of Southdown Leylands in preservation, but all three are fitted with different bodies. Nearest the camera is East Lancs, then follows Park Royal and Beadle, all superb manufacturers from Britain's past. There are only subtle differences between them all.

An unexpected photo of 1961 Harrington-bodied Leyland Leopard 2722 CD, which is seen parked by the old bus station in Haywards Heath in the early days of preservation. Whilst the bus station no longer exists the coach is very much active.

1961 Leyland Leopard L2 2726 CD with Harrington Cavalier coachwork seated just twenty-eight when new, creating a spacious interior for tour work. Fleet number 1726 was attending the Hellingly steam fair in 2019.

Leyland Leopard L2 2726 CD at Lewes bus rally in 2009. The stylish Harrington coachwork was built in Hove. Southdown was a loyal customer, purchasing many examples and often to their own specification.

749 DCD is a 1963 Leyland Leopard with Harrington Grenadier coachwork, another former touring coach that seated just twenty-eight. Beautifully restored, although preserved it does earn its keep in a revenue-earning capacity.

A rear view of 1963 Leyland Leopard 750 DCD, bodied by Harrington on Worthing seafront during the bus show in 2009. It was restored to a very high standard when part of the late Cyril Kenzie's collection and looks like new.

Harrington-bodied Leyland Leopard 750 DCD. Numbered 1750 with Southdown, this was a luxury twenty-eight-seat tourer, later joining sister coach 1749 in preservation. Its past life included tours of Scotland's islands and Highlands for a company using vintage and classic coaches.

KUF 199F, a Leyland Leopard new in January 1968, a year before the formation of the National Bus Company. The forty-five-seat Willowbrook body was delivered in traditional green and cream before adorning NBC green and white. It is photographed preserved in traditional livery.

KUF 199F, 199 in the Southdown fleet, was purchased for preservation directly from Southdown *c.* 1985. This was unusual as most vehicles for disposal would have been sold to dealers in large batches. 199 is always a very welcome sight at many rallies and shows. Photo taken at North Weald bus rally.

A rear view of Leyland Leopard KUF 199F parked on display at the Tinkers Park bus rally. One of a batch of fifteen Willowbrook-bodied Leopards new in 1968, this was the only one to survive from the batch and is always a pleasure to see at shows and rallies.

Two Leopards together. Of 165 Leyland Leopard buses purchased by Southdown, only four are known to survive, including Marshall-bodied 122 and Willowbrook-bodied 199 photographed at Amberley Museum bus show in 2009.

Amberley Museum in 2015. 1965 Leyland Leopard BUF 122C was sold by Southdown in 1977, being bought a little later by an operator in Ireland where it spent about ten years. Luckily, it was spotted unused but in poor condition and was purchased for preservation *c.* 2001. The rest is history.

I had the most enjoyable ride on Leyland Leopard BUF 122C in 2015, arriving at Uckfield for a photo shoot. This bus reminded me of Southdown in the 1970s when Leyland Leopards were commonplace in most bus companies.

The cab area of 1965 Leyland Leopard BUF 122C. It is very basic by today's standards but is typical of Leyland and Southdown for the time. It is half a century old – yes, fifty years – when I took these photos in 2015. A joy to see preserved.

It is easy to get carried away with the camera when you see something you like, and this was me enjoying Marshall-bodied Leyland Leopard 122 at Amberley Museum in 2015. Note the large luggage pens in this view and other period features.

An inside shot of Marshall-bodied 122 with a seating capacity of forty-five. A typical service bus of the 1960s and 1970s and the mainstay of most bus fleets all over the country. Southdown was no exception, operating 135 of them with three body types.

New in 1965, Leyland Leopard BUF 126C was preserved in the north of England and was regularly seen at shows and rallies. It also took a marching band to events in and around Lancashire. Disaster struck when it was heavily vandalised and was sadly scrapped in 1994.

The one that got away. Leyland Leopard EUF 140D was offered for sale by a Blackburn company *c.* 1990. Your author viewed the bus with the intention of purchasing for preservation, but regrettably I was not able to meet the asking price and 140 was scrapped in 1992 – a sad loss.

954 CUF is the first of the preserved Leyland PD3 Queen Mary double-deckers to feature in this book. 954 was new to Southdown in 1964 and was one of 285 such buses, the mainstay of double-deck operation for many years. 954 is seen at Worthing rally in 2008 having had a full restoration.

BUF 277C dates from 1965 and has an interesting past, like so many former Southdown buses. After disposal it worked for OK Motor Services of County Durham and became a driver training bus, also in the north. It is nice to see this one on home turf at Shoreham in 1997 and back in green and cream.

A tribute to Northern Counties bodybuilders of Wigan: Leyland PD3 Queen Mary 277 and Leyland Leopard 465. They supplied Southdown with around 330 examples of their work, two of which are seen here and are preserved.

972 CUF is a Queen Mary from the 1964 batch. I think it is pleasing to see a preserved bus on show at a rally in its acquired condition or partly restored. Photo taken in Southsea, 1999. For the record, 972 is now very smart in green and cream.

Queen Mary BUF 279C, like sister bus 277, was operated by OK Motor Services of County Durham. It eventually moved back south after a spell in Essex to join other Southdown vehicles in preservation. Photo taken at Showbus, Duxford, 1998.

Home again. 279 on Worthing seafront looking like it has had a fresh coat of green and cream. Corgi released a model of this bus in 2001 in the livery of past operator OK Motor Services.

From the 1966 batch of Leyland PD3 Queen Marys, FCD 286D is seen on display at Southsea in 2015. In acquired condition for preservation, it was formerly a driver training bus in the north-east after work with OK Motor Services. It has since been painted National green and white.

FCD 294D is a Queen Mary from the 1966 batch. Staying with Southdown after many Queen Marys had left the fleet, it has been a driver training bus in yellow livery and carried Stagecoach stripes. Now in preservation and back to the original green and cream.

1967 saw the last Queen Marys delivered to Southdown, nicknamed 'the Panoramics' due to their different window design. Twenty-four were received and three survive in preservation. HCD 347E is pictured at a wet Crowthorne rally in 1997.

Queen Mary HCD 356E attended the Southdown centenary event at Southsea in 2015 in its acquired condition, adding variety to the buses in preservation. The livery is of former owner Confidence of Leicester – spot the green showing through. 356 had also been a horse trials commentary box.

Formerly 401 DCD and one of thirty convertible open-top Leyland PD3 Queen Marys in the Southdown fleet new in 1964/65. Most of the convertibles lost their original registrations for transfer to coaches. 401 is seen at Southsea in 1992 with its roof on.

Reregistered back to its original registration number, 401 DCD is minus its roof, which is perfect for giving visitors to Amberley Museum a ride around the grounds. 401 was previously a driver training bus in Lancaster, returning south for preservation.

1964 Queen Mary 401 DCD is at Tinkers Park, Hadlow Down, 2015. The Southdown Queen Marys fitted with Northern Counties bodywork were full front, unlike other operators specifying half-cab for their double-deckers.

An irresistible photo opportunity at Amberley Museum. Queen Mary 403 DCD is sadly no longer around but the registration number lives on, carried by Stagecoach Enviro from 2010. An attractive view of the rear of Leyland PD2 RUF 186 from 1956.

Leyland PD3 Queen Mary 409 DCD from 1964 poses for the camera with Bristol FLF from 1966. The Bristol was new to Brighton Hove and District, becoming part of the Southdown fleet in 1969. It was operated by Top Deck Travel, whose livery it was in when acquired for preservation. It was seen regularly Hove *c.* 2002 but seems to have vanished from Sussex in recent years.

Convertible open-top Queen Mary 409 DCD has been fortunate to have a continuous life in preservation after service with Southdown and subsequent owner Stagecoach. I would say this is one of the most photographed preserved buses and something of a celebrity, attending many events in the south-east. Photo taken at North Weald bus rally.

Photographed by my daughter Laura in Southsea in May 2022, 409 DCD was looking new and decorated with balloons for a celebratory event. It was part of the Stagecoach heritage fleet at the time of writing. 409 was used for occasional work for hire and reward such as special events.

Another Queen Mary to lose its registration to a coach during the 1980s was 410 DCD, seen here in open-top form. It has had an interesting past having worked in London as a hop-on hop-off sightseeing bus, and once wore the yellow fleet colours of The Kings Ferry of Kent.

A Queen Mary in beautiful condition when photographed in July 2023. 416 DCD is on Worthing seafront taking part in the bus show. It is hard to believe these buses are getting close to sixty years old.

Two convertible open-top Queen Marys from 1964. Whilst 409 DCD is preserved in traditional green and cream in open-top form, DRR 153B (formerly 419 DCD) is preserved in National Bus Company green and white in closed-top form. Photo taken in Southsea in 1999.

DRR 153B lost its original registration (419 DCD) to a coach in the 1980s. 419 spent some of its career in Derbyshire as a driver trainer for Trent. Some modifications to the front and rear lights were carried out. Seen at Netley in 2019, it is a delightful change to see a bus preserved in National green and white.

Fast-forward around ten years and 419 is reunited with its original registration and has been restored, including the installation of correct lighting, painted white and preserved in the Newhaven area. The all-over white suits the Queen Mary and is its fifth colour scheme to date.

1964 Leyland PD3 Queen Mary 422 DCD in open-top form gives rides to Amberley Museum visitors at the autumn bus show in September 2014. Part of the destination display shows 'The Derby', a race attended every year by Southdown open-top buses.

A pair of Leylands caught by the camera whilst I was taking a ride on an open-top bus at Amberley Museum. 422, a 1964 Leyland PD3, and 122, a 1965 Leyland Leopard, are basking in the autumn sunshine. I wonder if these two were ever allocated to the same garage with Southdown.

AOR 156B, formerly 424 DCD, is one of two Queen Marys preserved by Southdown and acquired by Stagecoach with the takeover of Southdown. It was looking resplendent in green and cream minus its roof and carrying fleet number 3223, renumbered as part of the fully depreciated vehicle fleet.

Reunited with its original registration, 1964 Leyland PD3 424 DCD is photographed at Cosham in April 1996 with its roof on. It is looking good for its thirty-two years and is continually popular with enthusiasts all over the country.

424 DCD, seen with an open top once again. This Queen Mary is preserved by the long-established Essex company Stephenson's, retaining the traditional green and cream livery and carrying their fleet name in gold block, similar to Southdown's style.

From the 1965 delivery of Leyland PD3 Queen Marys is BUF 260C with Northern Counties body and a fixed roof. Having been in Cambridgeshire wearing a rather nice red and cream livery, it has returned to the south coast and is once again in green and cream. Photo taken at Duxford in 1994.

Queen Mary WRU 702B was formerly 406 DCD. I had some close association with three of these convertibles when I worked at Southdown and 406 was one of them. This photo was taken in 1988 when 406 had just been collected from Horsham directly from Southdown for preservation. (Thanks to Alan Elliott)

PUF 165H is one of a batch of thirty Leyland Leopards with Northern Counties dual-purpose bodies with a somewhat unique specification to Southdown and very similar to coaches. 465 was brought back from Ireland in the 1990s, preserved and repainted in National Bus Company green and white. Seen at Worthing garage in 1999.

One of two known survivors of the batch of thirty Northern Counties-bodied Leyland Leopards, both preserved. PUF 165H had just arrived on Maderia Drive, Brighton, for the seventy-fifth Brighton Hove and District rally. These were my favourite Southdown vehicles. Sadly, 465 has disappeared from the rally scene at the time of writing.

Southdown operated eighty-five Bristol REs with only three known survivors. TCD 481J and TCD 490J, from a batch of ten new in 1971 with forty-five-seat bodywork by Marshall of Cambridge, were at the Worthing bus rally in 2011.

TCD 481J at Amberley Museum in 2015. It is in lovely condition following restoration and a repaint to traditional Southdown green and cream, which it had from new. These buses were fitted with Leyland engines and due to their power they were initially allocated to the hilly routes in Brighton. It is wonderful to see 481 in preservation.

TCD 490J is at the Southsea rally in 1996. It is in the livery of Blue Lake, Chichester, who ran this after disposal by Southdown. After withdrawal by Blue Lake in 1996, it fortunately secured a preservation home and was restored to Southdown colours once again.

Worthing in 2011 and Bristol RE TCD 490J is on display, beautifully restored to Southdown original green and cream. The 1971 Bristol REs were the last Bristol single-decks purchased by the company. I remember 490 well when allocated to Haywards Heath depot during my time with Southdown.

UCD 602J was one of three 1971 Bristol RE buses bodied by Eastern Coach Works. The photo was taken *c.* 1992 at Kingscote station on the Bluebell Railway. Sadly 492 did not last long in preservation and it was scrapped in Barnsley *c.* 1993. None of the trio survived.

273 AUF is a Leyland Leopard with bodywork by Marshall that was new to Southdown in 1963. One of a batch of twenty-five, 673 is the only known survivor. It was sold to East Kent in *c.* 1971, which seemed a premature withdrawal from Southdown service. After only five years with East Kent, it was used in the Staffordshire area and acquired for preservation *c.* 1996.

273 AUF was acquired by enthusiasts from Kent for the well-deserved preservation and restoration. 673 was painted in East Kent colours, a company it worked for after disposal by Southdown. Looking magnificent, I photographed it at Tinkers Park bus rally in 2019 before a trip out in the Sussex countryside.

A delightful rear photo of Leyland Leopard 273 AUF preserved in East Kent colours, who operated it after Southdown. 673 was new in 1963. This photo could easily be from that era, but it was more like 2019 during the Tinkers Park bus rally and running day.

PPM 210G, a Bristol RE new to Brighton Hove and District in 1968, seen here looking wonderful after a repaint back to the livery it carried when new. After withdrawal by Southdown it was used in Somerset, also spending time in Dorset before returning to Sussex. Photo taken at Netley, near Southampton, in 1995.

New to Brighton Hove and District in 1968, PPM 210G, an Eastern Coach Works-bodied Bristol RE from a batch of ten, was inherited by Southdown with the business in 1969. I provided a temporary home in Sussex as previous accommodation had fallen through. Engineless and generally down at heel, it was sold to a Hampshire preservationist in 2013.

A rear view of Leyland National number 20, BCD 820L, seemingly in the condition it came out of service with Southdown and nicely preserved undercover with the Science Museum's collection. (My thanks to Tim Moss for use of his photo and the Science Museum for publication)

In June 2015 a gathering took place in Southsea to celebrate 100 years of Southdown. Looking impressive is Daimler Fleetline TCD 374J, new in 1970 with bodywork by Northern Counties. One of a batch of thirty new between 1970 and 1972, 374 is the only known survivor in the UK.

YCD 75T, a Leyland National new to Southdown in August 1978, is on display at Duxford bus show in 2008. 75 was acquired for preservation in P&O Ferries colours from its days working in Dover as a shuttle bus after withdrawal by Southdown.

Leyland National YCD 75T displaying a repaint at Alton bus rally in 2017. 75 is a twin-door bus and retains this configuration. Around 138 Nationals were bought new by Southdown between 1973 and 1982. Six are known to be in preservation.

PCD 80R is a Leyland National new to Southdown in 1977. It is owned by a good friend of mine who has had a thorough restoration carried out on the bus, and the result is amazing. Photo taken at Tinkers Park in 2015, where it is ready to take passengers on a trip to Heathfield.

This view of Leyland National PCD 80R Southdown fleet number 34 was taken at Tinkers Park bus show. The very high standard of presentation is evident. Note the addition to the livery: 'Let Southdown show you beautiful Britain', the inspiration for which came from wording once carried on a Queen Mary bus in the 1980s.

34 poses for the camera at Tinkers Park bus show. Eastbourne was its allocated depot at Southdown. It is back on home territory in preservation, reliving some of the old routes once run by the company. This view shows the 'beautiful Britain' sign writing on the opposite side from the last view.

A close-up rear view of Leyland National 34 with amazing artwork and attention to detail with the restoration and continued preservation. It is a very active vehicle, attending many bus shows, running days and other events during the season.

Well-travelled National RUF 37R was sold by Southdown *c.* 1987 to Rennies of Dunfermline. It returned south when acquired by Provincial in Hampshire and was later bought by a preservationist. Seen at Ardingly steam rally in 2009 in all-over green.

After some fourteen years in preservation, 37 was photographed at the Worthing bus show in July 2023 looking superb with a repaint complete with white band. New in February 1977, this Leyland National was forty-six years old when this shot was taken.

Leyland National AYJ 97T was new to Southdown in 1979. A very smart fifty-two seater with single-door layout and cloth-covered seats as opposed to the vinyl seats of the older ones. Seen here at Tinkers Park in 2019 for the bus show painted green and cream to replicate the return of these colours in 1986.

AYJ 97T arriving at Amberley and turning at the railway station before entering the museum grounds for the spring bus show in April 2023. Leyland Nationals such as 97 were a familiar sight on our roads in the 1970s and 1980s, with over 7,000 built.

A rear view of 97 on display at the Amberley Museum bus show in April 2023. Looking as though it has gained an original engine-access flap, many were modified by Southdown to create advertising space. I am sure this batch had rear route numbers, which was unusual for Leyland Nationals but requested by Southdown.

SCD 731N is a Leyland Atlantean with Park Royal bodywork new to Southdown in 1974. After Southdown it worked as far as Liverpool and Manchester before securing a preservation home back on the south coast. 731 is the only known survivor from a batch of forty-six. It is seen here at a Worthing bus rally.

A811 CCD, a 1984 Leyland Tiger, was owned by your author when this photo was taken in 2007 at the Duxford bus rally. It was its first outing since being repainted and having original exterior lighting installed. I was the proud winner of the Best Single-Deck From the 1980s award, mainly for originality, which is not always easy to achieve when restoring a vehicle.

A811 CCD is on display on Maderia Drive, Brighton, in June 2010, taking part in Brighton Hove and District's seventy-fifth anniversary. It'd recently had 'National Holidays' vinyls applied, which she carried when new in 1984. The bodywork is by Duple and only six were bought by Southdown for tour work.

Leyland Tiger A811 CCD in attendance at the Detling bus and coach show in March 2012. My attempt to achieve as much authenticity in the restoration as possible saw the reinstatement of original exterior lighting and badges, which was rewarding when comparing to photos I have when new in 1984.

Originality is often hard to achieve in preservation, but this Duple laser bodywork retained its original features, apart from the added tables and blue rear seats, which was an error at the trimmers. I photographed the interior of A811 CCD after a cleaning frenzy.

A rear of my Tiger parked up at Southdown PSV in West Sussex *c.* 2012. Trying to replicate the original look from when it was new in 1984, I sourced original lighting for the rear, a mud flap with Duple stickers and badges too.

Sadness struck in 2013 when I had to reluctantly part with A811 CCD after a few years of enjoyment; it was like losing a best friend. In this photo its in the Derbyshire area, reregistered and pretending to be a Trent coach. At the time of writing, I hear it has returned to the south coast for continued preservation.

The second 1971 Leyland Leopard preserved from the original batch of twenty-five new in that year is 1835 (UUF 335J). It is on display at Duxford show bus rally in 2006 sporting a later Plaxton front end from a Supreme. Carrying the traditional green livery, it nicely represents that era of coaching, as does sister bus 1828.

This Eastbourne Pullman was aptly named as 1835 was allocated to Southdown's Eastbourne depot. When new this batch was used on tour work and has doubtless been to many holiday destinations during their time with Southdown. Photo taken at Southsea in 2015.

UUF 335J is a well-travelled coach. After Southdown it was owned by operators in Yorkshire, Tyne and Wear and Cumbria, and its preservation homes include Essex and Berkshire. It is over half a century old in this view at Amberley Museum bus show in April 2023.

A rear view of UUF 335J on display at Amberley Museum grounds in April 2023. It displays the Eastbourne town council crest as a tribute to its part in serving the town for many years. EFE produced a model of a Southdown Plaxton Elite which was released in 1994.

PUF 249M is a 1974 Ford with Duple Dominant coach work. I have a fondness for Ford coaches, and from a batch of forty bought by Southdown this is the only one known to survive. Living in the north of Scotland since *c.* 1996, its on my list for a visit one day.

KIB 7027 was formerly EAP 937V, a 12-metre-long Leyland Leopard with Duple bodywork. It is from a batch of four Southdown purchased in 1979 for general coach work. It is seen here on display at Duxford show bus rally in 2005 in her previous operator's livery from Merseyside.

A coach with a chequered history. MAP 340W, a 1981 Plaxton-bodied Leyland Leopard, is seen at the show bus rally at Duxford in 2007. It's looking remarkable in the London to Gatwick livery, a replication of her service with Southdown. I recall photographing it in Wales after disposal in a bland light blue colour. This restoration is superb.

Though not new to Southdown, Bristol VR LFS 296F is nevertheless a worthy inclusion. New in 1968, it was one of eight acquired from Eastern Scottish in exchange for Bristol Lodekkas in 1973. I came across it on a visit to the Keighley Bus Museum in May 2022 in Alder Valley colours where she was used as an open-topper.

Bristol VR 510 UUF 110J was new in 1971 and was one of a great many of this type with bodywork by Eastern Coach Works of Lowestoft. I provided 510 with overnight accommodation at Southdown PSV after having had some restoration – a welcome sight for me. Incidentally, the Dennis Dart next to it is now preserved too.

Most buses have an interesting past and Bristol VR UUF 116J is no exception. Sold by Southdown to Crosville in Wales, it was later bought by Mersey Tunnels who removed the roof and used it as a mobile maintenance platform. An ambitious preservationist purchased it and undertook restoration, even replacing the roof – a super job done. Photo taken at Amberley Museum.

GNJ 583N, a Bristol VR from the 1975 Southdown order, is from a small batch of five with Leyland engines instead of the more standard Gardner units. 583 once wore Brighton and Hove red and cream. In this view at Southsea in 2015 preparation is underway for the application of National Bus Company's green and white.

Another bus brought back south for preservation after use in the north is GNJ 583N, a 1975 Bristol VR. It is seen here showing off a partly restored Eastern Coach Works bodywork at Southsea in 2015, celebrating 100 years of Southdown.

Dual doors and a convertible open top are a rare combination This is the specification of Bristol VR TPN 103S, on display at the Worthing bus show in July 2023. 603 was its fleet number with Southdown and its preservation home is in the Brighton area.

Bristol VR UWV 614S, nicknamed *Frankie*, has been preserved in Devon for many years, retaining the River Link colours from its previous service life. 614 takes part in many rallies and running days. It was at Kingsbridge for the running day in September 2023 in open-top form.

A rear view of Bristol VR UWV 614S in Plymouth, August 2019, for the running day. 614 is a convertible open-top Bristol VR bus, one of thirty bought by Southdown in 1977 and 1978. *Frankie*, as its fondly known, has spent more time in the West Country than it did with Southdown on the south coast.

EAP 984V is a Bristol VR new to Southdown in 1980. In this view at the Worthing bus rally it is seen repainted in National green and white, as it was when new. 684 had an all-over advert for *Evening Argus* and has worn Stagecoach's corporate striped livery.

EAP 984V appearing in full Midland Fox livery was a surprise. It is seemingly now preserved in the Midlands. I have to say, 684 does look rather smart. (My thanks to Andrew Chambers for use of his photo, taken in Wythall in April 2022)

The last batch of Bristol VRs to be delivered to Southdown were twenty-seven from 1981. JWV 266W has previously been in Stagecoach stripes, then plain white for a firm in Hampshire. Seen at Tinkers Park bus rally in 2015 and restored to Southdown green and cream.

JWV 272W, a Bristol VR from the 1981 batch, is at Duxford show bus rally in 2007. 272 was part of the Brighton and Hove fleet from 1986 and was painted in two variations of their livery. It has also been all-over white in the Buckinghamshire area and is now looking the part in National Bus Company green and white.

Bristol VR JWV 275W, a former Brighton to Portsmouth 700 service bus with Southdown, now represents the National Bus Company era in green and white, just as 275 was when new. This batch from 1981 is popular in preservation. Photo taken at the Cobham bus rally in 2007.

Numerically the last Bristol VR purchased by Southdown in 1981. JWV 976W is painted in a commemorative livery based on the traditional green and cream of old, and suits the Eastern Coach Works body. 276 is on display at Amberley Museum in 2005.

A twin-door Bristol VR that was bodied by Eastern Coach Works and bought by Southdown in 1977 primarily for busy Brighton town centre routes. Transferred to Brighton and Hove in 1986, UFG 625S is preserved and was in store when this photo was taken in 2009.

Bristol VR AAP 651T is seen at Southsea in 2015 for the Southdown centenary. Another well-travelled bus with an interesting history, 651 passed to Brighton and Hove in 1986 and has worked in Oxfordshire, Lancashire and North Wales.

Bristol VR AAP 651T now resides back on the south coast in preservation and is beautifully restored in Stagecoach 729 livery for the Brighton to Tunbridge Wells service, which it wore with Southdown. Photo taken in Worthing in July 2023.

Side view of a topless Bristol VR UWV 617S at Amberley Museum grounds. 617 has worked in various parts of the UK since its Southdown days including Scotland, Gloucestershire, Scotland again and Cornwall, appearing in about seven different liveries.

A nice frontal view of Bristol VR UWV 617S at Amberley Museum, one of thirty convertible open-toppers. 617 is very well presented with a stunning repaint in Southdown green and cream, West Sussex fleet names and a nicely set destination display.

Preserved open-top Bristol VR UWV 617S pauses at Buxted railway station in East Sussex whilst taking part in the Tinkers Park bus rally and running day with your author enjoying a ride out. It's always a joy to travel on buses that have been painstakingly restored by their owners.

Whilst some former Southdown convertible open-top Bristol VRs have been sold to owners overseas, UWV 617S has a preservation home in the south. Here is a rear view of it at Uckfield whilst taking part in the Tinkers Park bus running day and rally.

Before the heavens opened at Worthing as the buses assembled for the show on 30 July 2023, I managed another picture of Bristol VR UWV 617S. The standard of presentation achieved by preservationists is high, and 617 is no exception.

A magnificent line-up at Southsea bus show in 1990, with an impressive eleven green and creams in a row. Most of these vehicles continue in preservation and attend rallies and shows during the season. From the oldest to the newest is somewhere in the region of sixty years.

Preserving history. My most recent visit to Amberley Museum in West Sussex was in April 2023. Inside one of the Southdown garages were two Leyland Titans from the 1930s and a 1914 Tilling Stevens in the middle. A wonderful display!

The former Southdown bus garage from Storrington at Amberley Museum. Southdown had a great many garages of differing sizes depending on vehicle allocation, and open parking facilities too. I would estimate it peaked to somewhere around fifty. Some still exist with different uses. It is pleasing to see this one preserved.

'Southdown in preservation' is not just about preserving the buses and coaches, but all the other associated memorabilia too. Like many other enthusiasts I have a collection of leaflets and timetables produced by Southdown over the years. This fare table is from 1959 and cost me more than a shilling when I bought it thirty years after it was published.

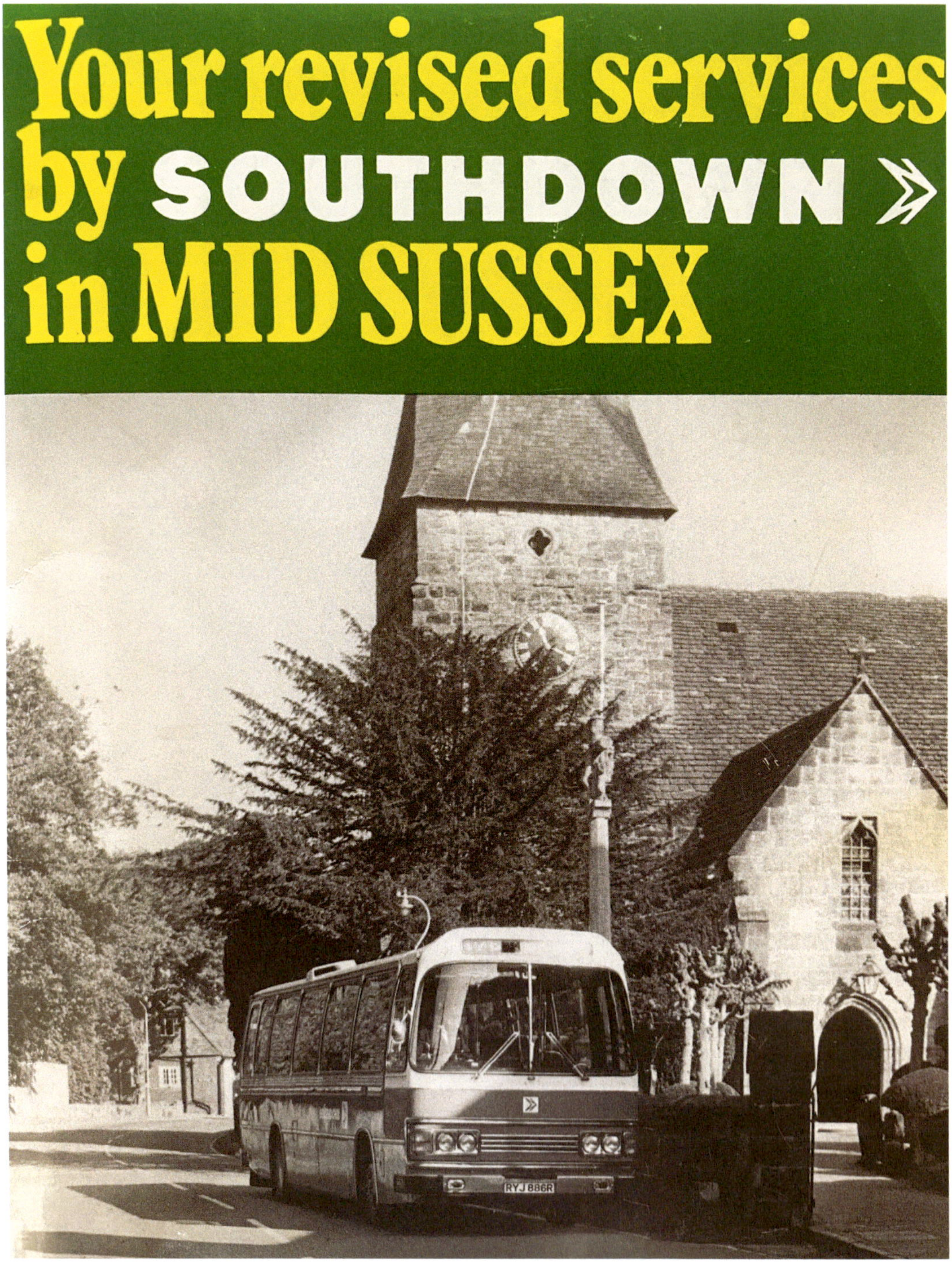

Bus and coach services changed a lot in the 1980s; some improved, but many were reduced. The photo on this Mid Sussex Revised Services leaflet is taken by Lindfield church, an area I know well. Leyland Leopard dual-purpose coach RYJ 886R is passing the church, a vehicle that is sadly not preserved.

A selection of leaflets from the Haywards Heath area. When these were produced I lived in the town and worked for Southdown at their garage there. Preserving the history of a great company and sharing the memories.

Ten Volvo double-deckers with bodywork by Northern Counties of Wigan were delivered in 1989. These were the last new buses ordered by Southdown. They went into service in green and cream. When Stagecoach took over Southdown they adopted their striped livery. F308 MYJ is at Southsea in 2015 in its previous operator's livery and private registration.

It is very sad to see old buses languishing in yards, but I came across former Southdown Volvo F310 MYJ in September 2022. Regrettably not preserved as far as I am aware, but notable as 310 was numerically the last bus delivered to Southdown. Hopefully it will find a home.

It's not just buses that get preserved, but also the history of the company and their vehicles. DLK 292C helps us do this. A 1965 AEC Mammoth Major fuel tanker once used by Southdown, it has had a thorough restoration by owner John Murphy. (My thanks to John for use of the photo)

TSU 352, an AEC Matador bought by Southdown for recovery use *c.* 1973. The vehicle was rebuilt using bus parts, and some are easily recognisable. It is seen nicely preserved and on show at the Worthing bus rally in July 2023.

I wanted to include some buses from the operating area of Southdown that are preserved. 23 ACD was new to Brighton Corporation in 1963. A Leyland PD2 with bodywork by Weymann, it is seen taking part in the Worthing bus rally in July 2023.

Preserved former Brighton Hove and District is this Bristol KSW with Eastern Coach Works bodywork dating from 1953. It is seen sat outside its former depot at Conway Street, Hove, in 1993, forty years after being built.

Just arrived at Tinkers Park bus rally in East Sussex is BJK 672D, a 1966 Leyland PD2 with East Lancashire Coachbuilders' bodywork, a preserved Eastbourne bus. The blue and yellow is as pleasing to the eye as Southdown green and cream.

I have had many enjoyable visits to Amberley Museum over the years and taken many photographs. I was caught by the camera this time amongst the superb collection of Southdown archive material in one of the garages. Every picture tells a story.

I had to include my wife, who enjoys my hobby too and accompanies me to many bus shows and railway events. This shot at Tinkers Park is of Leyland National PCD 34R, owned by a good friend of mine, Paul Lewellyn. My wife and I are about to take a trip to Heathfield.

Acknowledgements

Whilst I have a large photograph collection of Southdown buses and coaches there are always some that I do not have that I want to include. Fellow enthusiasts are always willing to help provide that elusive photo or slide. Therefore, my sincere thanks goes to Michael Taylor, Steve Cockram, Alan Elliott, Tim Moss and Andrew Chambers. My thanks also to Amberley Museum for allowing publication of photos taken there and to the Science Museum for allowing publication of photos taken at their site in Wiltshire. Thank you to anyone I may have missed, and apologies if I have.

Contents

All routes described in this guide have been recently walked by the author and both the author and publisher have made all reasonable efforts to ensure that all information is as accurate as possible. However, while a printed book remains constant for the life of an edition, things in the countryside often change. Trails are subject to forces outside our control: for example, landslides, tree-falls or other matters can result in damage to paths or route changes; waymarks and signposts may fade or be destroyed by wind, snow or the passage of time; or trails may not be maintained by the relevant authorities. If you notice any discrepancies between the contents of this guide and the facts on the ground, then please let us know. Our contact details can be found at the back of this book.

Getting Help

Emergency Services Number: **dial 112 or 118**

Distress Signal

The signal that you are in distress is 6 blasts on a whistle spaced over a minute, followed by a minute's silence. Then repeat. The response that your signal has been received is 3 blasts of a whistle over a minute followed by a minute's silence. At night, flashes of a torch can also be used in the same sequences. **Always carry a torch and whistle.**

Signalling to a Helicopter from the Ground

Help Required

Raise both arms in the shape of a 'Y'

Help Not Required

Raise one arm and extend the other arm down and outwards

WARNING

Hills and mountains can be dangerous places and walking is a potentially dangerous activity. Many of the routes described in this guide cross exposed and potentially hazardous terrain. You walk entirely at your own risk. It is solely your responsibility to ensure that you and all members of your group have adequate experience, fitness and equipment. Neither the author nor the publisher accepts any responsibility or liability whatsoever for death, injury, loss, damage or inconvenience resulting from use of this book, participation in the activity of mountain walking or otherwise.

Some land may be privately owned so we cannot guarantee that there is a legal right of entry to the land. Occasionally, routes change as a result of land disputes.

The sublime descent to Rifugio Pian de Fontana (Stage 10)

Introduction

Prayer flags near Forcella de Zita Sud (Stage 10)

The Dolomites

There is something very special about the Italian Dolomites. Although they are immediately adjacent to the main Alpine chain, they are different. Very different. Different in shape. Different in colour. And most importantly from a trekker's point of view, different in atmosphere and aura. Of these peculiarities, the unique shape of these magnificent mountains is most instantly obvious: the sharp pointy peaks (with their jagged and often seemingly impossible angles), spiky broken crests and incredibly sheer cliffs and walls, are unlike those in any other range. And the colour of the Dolomites is striking too: they are made of limestone and are known as the 'Pale Mountains' for good reason. The rock here varies in shade from pale grey to an unforgettable bright white which takes on a sublime pink hue at sunrise and sunset.

However, it is the aura of the Dolomites which will shape your experience the most and leave you yearning to return. This ambiance is less tangible than the mere physical appearance of the peaks but you will feel it more strongly each day as you wander through the plateaus and valleys of these incomparable mountains. Of course the sheer beauty of the surroundings provides the foundations for these feelings, but other factors shape them. The sad history of the region certainly has a part to play: the Dolomites served as the arena for much fighting during World War 1 (WW1). Many of the paths you walk were military 'roads' built during this period and other evidence of the conflict is still on display in the form of bunkers and tunnels. As is often the case in the best stories, beauty and sorrow combine for an evocative and memorable experience.

The cultural characteristics of the Dolomites also shape the experience. In the northern sections, often German is the first language and the southern sections are largely Italian-speaking. The cultures of these two zones are very different and this is most apparent from the different foods served at the huts (see 'Food' below). Indeed, the food is particularly wonderful in the Italian areas. So good in fact that we would argue that the AV1 offers the finest culinary experience of any trek in the world. If that is not enough to persuade you to visit, then we do not know what is!

The AV1

The AV1 is the premier long-distance trekking route in the Dolomites, normally taking between 6 and 11 days. It is the perfect way to explore the range's exquisite beauty and its fascinating open-air museum of WW1 history. It is a linear route, entirely within Italy, between Lago di Braies in the north and Belluno in the south. On the journey, you cross incredible high mountain passes enabling travel from magnificent valley to magnificent valley: a pass is known as a 'forcella' or 'passo' in Italian. And there are exquisite alpine plateaus, wonderful grassy pastures and carpets of wild-flowers, the like of which you will never have seen before.

Distance	121km
Altitude Gain/ Loss	7,207m/ 8,248m
Days	6 to 11
Highest Point	Rifugio Lagazuoi (2752m)

You will live and breathe these scenic delights, night and day, because you need never leave the mountains. Unlike some alpine treks, the AV1 never enters villages or hamlets: fabulous accommodation is available in remote mountain huts cleverly spaced out along the route. Places with views that most people dream of but few will ever see. Places that you will never forget. Places that will leave you with remarkable memories. This is, without a doubt, a trek that should be on your bucket list.

Although the AV1 is popular, it rarely feels as busy as some other treks such as the Tour du Mont Blanc (TMB). This huge swathe of the Dolomites is easily large enough to swallow the many walkers that descend upon it each summer. Get a reasonably early start and you will find yourself largely alone for much of the day. You will occasionally pass, or be passed by, other trekkers but these meetings can be as fleeting as you wish. And at the end of the day, on arrival at your resting place, often high above the valleys, you will likely meet some of the people you came across during the day. Then bonds are formed over dinner or a drink. Like the TMB, the AV1 has a fine reputation as a sociable trek.

'AV' stands for 'Alta Via' which means 'High Route' in English. The AV1 is the first, and most popular, of a number of such Alte Vie in the Dolomites. Notwithstanding statistics published elsewhere, we find the main AV1 route to be 121km in length with 7,207 metres of ascent and 8,248 metres of descent. In addition, there are some incredible variants described here in detail: they are summarised in a separate table in the Itinerary Planner.

If the statistics sound intimidating then do not worry: with the right preparation, planning and approach, the AV1 is perfectly manageable for most people of reasonable fitness. Yes it is a challenge but it is an achievable one. And that is where this guidebook comes in! Most of what you need to know to prepare for the AV1 is here within these pages. And the entire route is described in detail to guide you on the trek itself. Furthermore, unlike other books, this one contains Real Maps: for each stage, there is a 1:25,000 scale map, licensed from the relevant mapping agency.

How hard is the AV1?

The AV1 is a multi-day trek with significant distances to travel, and metres to climb, each day. Accordingly, a reasonable level of fitness is required. However, it is fair to say that it is far from the most difficult trek in the Alps and it is therefore an excellent option for those new to trekking. The overall distance is short compared to some other Alpine treks. And unlike some other treks, once you are 'up' you stay 'up': the AV1 rarely dips below 1500m. Of course there are climbs and descents, but there are fewer of the huge climbs experienced elsewhere.

The sensible spacing of the mountain huts ('rifugi') helps too: it is simple to design an itinerary to suit your own specific abilities. And, with a few exceptions, the AV1 is well-served by good paths and tracks: there are some sections which are more challenging but they can all be bypassed if required. Furthermore, if you walk in the conventional direction (N to S), the most difficult sections of the trek are undertaken towards the end when you are 'trail-hardened'. In summary, if you are reasonably fit then this trek should be within your capabilities.

Many who have completed the TMB (the most famous Alpine trek) look to the AV1 for their next trekking experience. Accordingly, it can be useful to compare these two treks. Although they are normally completed over a similar number of days, the AV1 is shorter (121km compared to 174km) and has less climbing (7,200m compared to 9,700m). On paper therefore, the AV1 is arguably the easier undertaking. However, the terrain on some short sections of the AV1 is a little more challenging than that on the TMB (see 'Paths and Waymarking' below).

Ask the Author

If you have any questions which are not answered by this book, then you can ask the author on our Facebook Group, **'Dolomites AV1'**

A special sunrise at Rifugio Carestiato (Stage 8a)

Direction and Start/Finish Points

The AV1 starts at Lago di Braies and finishes at Bolzano Bellunese near Belluno. Traditionally it is walked N to S and, as the vast majority travel that way, this book describes it in that direction. Although it could also be tackled S to N, there are some good reasons why few people do that. Firstly, the southern extremity of the trek is more than 1000m lower in altitude than Lago di Braies in the N: so if you head S, you have more downhill walking than uphill. If you walk N, then you have an additional 1000m of climbing.

Secondly, by walking S you face many of the most exposed and difficult sections towards the end of the trek, by which time your body has adjusted physically to the rigours of the trail and you are mentally better-prepared for the more serious exposure and difficulty.

Nevertheless, some people do undertake it S to N and that approach is not without merit: some prefer not to meet the same people every day and walking against the flow solves this problem. The Real Maps in this book, with numbered waypoints, make the route descriptions simple to follow in reverse.

It is also possible to walk shorter sections of the AV1. There are a number of access points along the route where you could leave or join the trek using public transport or taxis. These include Rifugio Pederü (Stage 2b), Passo Falzàrego (near Rifugio Lagazuoi and Cortina d'Ampezzo; Stage 3), Rifugio Scoiattoli (Stage 4c), Passo Giau (Stage 5a), Passo Staulanza (Stage 6a), Passo Duran (Stage 8b; no public transport) and Malga di Pramperet (just off the route of Stage 9). You could start at any of these places and walk a few sections. Or you could skip sections by leaving the route at one of these access points.

Staging Points

Public transport in the Dolomites can be infrequent so most people travel to the region the day before the trek and overnight close to the start at Lago di Braies. This provides an opportunity to organise your gear and stock up on food: there are no shops on the AV1. For travel arrangements to the staging points, see 'Travel' below.

The usual staging points include:

Lago di Braies/Pragser Wildsee: the hotel here has a magnificent setting and the AV1 starts right next to it. There is no supermarket at the lake so stock up on supplies before travelling there. The hotel books up fast and sometimes requires a 3-night stay so, in fact, most people stay elsewhere. As an alternative, there are hotels in San Vito which is one bus stop before Lago di Braies.

Villabassa/Niederdorf: this little town is on the train lines from Verona and Munich. It is only 20min by bus from Lago di Braies. It has hotels, shops and supermarkets.

Dobbiaco/Toblach: a lovely town with mountain views which is also on the train lines from Verona and Munich. By bus, it is 30min to Lago di Braies (via Villabassa) and 45min from Cortina d'Ampezzo. It has hotels, restaurants, shops and supermarkets.

Cortina d'Ampezzo: a bustling mountain resort with plenty of hotels, restaurants, shops and supermarkets. It is 2.5hr by bus from Venice Airport/Venice Mestre. Travel to Lago di Braies by bus takes about 1.5hr (including the change in Dobbiaco). Some prefer to overnight in Dobbiaco as you can get to Lago di Braies earlier the next morning.

Guided Tours, Self-Guided Tours or Independent Walking?

The question we get asked the most is whether to walk independently or with a guided group. The answer is a personal one, depending upon your own particular circumstances and requirements. For many, the decision to organise the trek themselves, and to walk independently, can be almost life-changing, opening the door for more difficult challenges in the future. There is much satisfaction to be gained in planning and navigating a trek yourself and the sense of achievement on completion is to be savoured.

In theory, most could walk independently: the AV1 is within the capabilities of most reasonably fit people and the trails are generally well-marked so, in normal conditions, route-finding is largely straightforward. However, the independent trekker usually carries his own pack and is responsible for all decisions which need to be made daily such as pacing; which way to go at junctions; when to stock up with food and water; and choice of route in bad weather. For some, this will be too great a burden on top of the physical effort required simply to walk the route. For those walkers, a guided group is a great solution: the tour company typically organises food, accommodation and (if possible) transfer of luggage each night. And the guide makes all the decisions, enabling the walker to concentrate on the walking. There are a number of tour companies operating guided trips on the AV1.

Self-guided tours are a popular middle-ground. The tour company books all the accommodation and provides all the advice and information required to complete the trek. However, the trekker walks the trail without a guide and normally carries his/her own pack. Many confident trekkers (who would be perfectly capable of walking independently) book a self-guided trip simply to avail of the accommodation booking service. Unlike the TMB, there is no central booking website where a number of different huts can be booked at once. On the AV1, independent trekkers need to book each hut separately and some find this to be a time-consuming and frustrating process (see 'Accommodation' below). By booking a self-guided tour, the stress and hassle are alleviated, albeit at a price.

The descent from Rifugio Tissi (Stage 7b)

When to go

Normally the AV1 can be tackled from late June to late September.

Late June can be a very beautiful time for walking. The weather is sunny and warm and the peaks are very photogenic, still fully-frosted with snow. Summer haze has not yet arrived so visibility is generally excellent with wide-ranging views. And there are carpets of spring wild-flowers. Of course, there is occasionally rain at this time of year but this usually lessens as the month progresses. And there are fewer visitors so accommodation is easier to find and significantly, the mountains are more peaceful. That said, trekking is becoming more and more popular so the number of early-season walkers seems to increase each year.

As with all Alpine treks, in some years, high passes can be snow-covered until early July, making parts of the AV1 difficult and/or dangerous: in such conditions, crampons and/or an ice axe might be helpful. There are now some very light and compact crampons available which weigh a mere 300g so carrying them just in case is not the burden it once was. Microspikes are another lightweight option for early-season trekkers.

July and August is the main summer season when the high passes are normally free of snow. It can be hot, sometimes reaching more than 30°C. Mornings often start with clear, sunny skies and heat up as the sun gains height. If there is to be cloud or haze, often this will arrive in the afternoon when thunderstorms are more likely. Start walking early in the morning to complete the main climb while the temperature is cooler. This is the busiest time on the AV1 and it is advisable to make bookings well in advance as accommodation is often full, particularly at weekends. Do not turn up without a reservation and expect to find accommodation. Furthermore, in this period, it can be difficult to alter your plans once on the trek: a change to one day's schedule has a chain reaction across the rest of your trip and huts may not be able to accommodate the changes.

Month	Pros	Cons
Late June	Pleasant temperatures Frequent sunny skies Good visibility Wild-flower season Fewer visitors	High passes occasionally inaccessible due to snow
July/August	Generally fine weather High passes normally accessible Basking in the sun!	The hottest period Sometimes hazy Visitor numbers highest Afternoon thunderstorms
September	Pleasant temperatures Frequent sunny skies Excellent visibility Fewer visitors Autumn colours	Accommodation closes as the month progresses Shorter days Cooler evenings Occasional snowfall

September is the new June! It can be the best month for walking as the weather is often more settled than in summer. Skies are usually clear and visibility excellent. Daytime temperatures are normally still warm but evenings get cooler and the days get shorter. The odd flurry of snow is possible (with the risk increasing as the month progresses) but they tend to clear quickly. It used to be that visitor numbers reduced dramatically when the Italian holidays finished at the end of August so that the mountains were significantly quieter and there was much less demand for accommodation. Nowadays, with the increased popularity of the AV1, this phenomenon is less pronounced and huts are frequently full to capacity even in September. However, it is still fair to say that the number of trekkers decreases, and bookings become easier, as September progresses. Nevertheless, it is still wise to book in advance. Towards the end of the month, accommodation starts to close for the season.

The easy track at the start of Stage 8a

Magnificent scenery on the descent to Rifugio Vazzoler (Stage 7b)

Using this Book

This book is designed to be used by walkers of differing abilities. Many guidebooks for long-distance treks rigidly divide the route into a fixed number of long day stages, leaving it up to the walker to break down those stages to design daily routes which suit his/her abilities. This book, however, has been laid out differently to give the trekker flexibility: it divides the route into 20 shorter sub-stages which can be combined to design daily routes to meet your own specific needs.

Each of the 20 sub-stages covers the distance between one accommodation option and the subsequent one. Almost every accommodation option on the entire route is the start/finish point of a sub-stage. You can choose how many of these sub-stages you wish to walk each day. Each sub-stage has its own walk description, route map, elevation profile and beautiful photos.

The labelling of the sub-stages uses a combination of numbers and letters. It is a simple system but requires a little bit of explanation. Firstly, every sub-stage has a number between 1 and 11: each number represents one day of our standard 11-day schedule. As the standard 11-day schedule is broken down into sub-stages, these sub-stages are also given letters (e.g. "6a"). Take a look at the detailed Itinerary Planner below and all should become clear.

The Itinerary Planner includes a range of tables outlining Suggested Itineraries of 6, 7, 8, 9, 10 and 11 days. In each table, the maths have been done for you so there is no need for you to waste time (and mental strength!) working out daily distances, timings and height gain.

Of course, the Suggested Itineraries are only suggestions. You can shorten or lengthen your day in any number of ways to suit yourself: just decide how many sub-stages you want to walk that day. It is up to you. As there is accommodation at the end of each sub-stage, it is easy to design your own bespoke itinerary and adjust it on the ground as you go along.

For example, day 6 of the standard 11-day route involves walking sub-stages 6a and 6b. But you could decide to extend day 6 by walking sub-stages 6a, 6b and 7a all on the same day. Or you might be tired and decide to shorten your day by walking only sub-stage 6a. With some other guidebooks, you would have to work out how to split stages yourself, involving some complicated maths to plan distances and times going forward. This guide, however, does all the hard mental work for you.

In this book:

Timings indicate the approximate time required by a reasonably fit walker to complete a sub-stage. They do not include stoppage time. Do not get frustrated if your own times do not match ours: everyone walks at different speeds. As you progress through the trek, you will soon learn how your own times compare with those given here and you will adjust your plans accordingly.

Distance is measured in kilometres (km) to match maps and signposts in Europe. One mile equates to 1.6km.

Ascent or descent numbers are the aggregate of all the altitude gain or loss (measured in metres) on the uphill or downhill sections of a sub-stage. As a rule of thumb, a fit walker climbs 300 to 400m in an hour.

Elevation profiles tell you where the climbs and descents fall on the route. The profile lines have been deliberately drawn in varying thickness purely for aesthetic purposes. Read the elevations off the top of the lines.

Place names are sometimes given in two languages, Italian and German (see 'Italian or German?' below).

Place names in brackets in the route descriptions indicate the direction to be followed on signposts. For example, "('Coldai')" would mean that you follow a sign for Coldai.

Real maps are provided. These are extracts from 1:25,000 scale maps produced by Tabacco. The route of the trek is marked on the maps.

The following abbreviations are used:

AV1	Alta Via 1
TMB	Tour du Mont Blanc
WW1	World War 1
TL	Turn left
TR	Turn right
SH	Straight ahead
N, S, E and W, etc.	North, South, East and West, etc.

The terrace at Rifugio Tissi (Stage 7a)

Itinerary Planner

Stage 10 is the wildest section of the AV1

Stage	Start	Time (hr)	Km	Ascent (m)	Descent (m)	Max. Altitude (m)
1	Lago di Braies	3.25	6.9	929	96	2389
2a	Rifugio Biella	1.00	3.1	53	264	2327
2b	Rifugio Sennes	1.75	4.8	0	568	2116
2c	Rifugio Pederü	2.00	5.2	560	48	2060
3	Rifugio Fanes	5.50	12.7	1069	377	2752
4a	Rifugio Lagazuoi	2.50	6.7	98	813	2752
4b	Rifugio Dibona	1.75	4.5	408	308	2137
4c	Rifugio Cinque Torri	1.25	2.2	438	0	2575
5a	Rifugio Nuvolau	1.50	2.5	60	399	2575
5b	Passo Giau	4.00	10.6	386	704	2357
6a	Rifugio Città di Fiume	1.00	3.1	56	208	1918
6b	Rifugio Passo Staulanza	2.50	6.8	528	162	2132
7a	Rifugio Coldai	2.50	4.7	435	317	2250
7b	Rifugio Tissi	1.75	5.9	75	611	2250
8a	Rifugio Vazzoler	3.75	9.3	627	507	1933
8b	Rifugio Bruto Carestiato	0.75	2.4	29	262	1834
9	Passo Duran	4.00	11.4	651	395	1966
10	Rifugio Pramperet	3.25	6.4	550	775	2451
11a	Rifugio Pian de Fontana	2.00	5.8	255	642	1740
11b	Rifugio Bianchet	1.75	6.1	0	792	1245
Finish	La Pissa					

Suggested Itineraries

Pale limestone peaks on Stage 9

11 Days: Option A

Our standard schedule which successfully divides the trek up into manageable stages. It is a tried and tested approach which is perfect for many walkers. Day 1 is a long, steep climb but there is no way around that, whatever your itinerary.

Day	Stages	Time (hr)	Km	Ascent (m)	Descent (m)
1	1	3.25	6.9	929	96
2	2a, 2b, 2c	4.75	13.1	613	880
3	3	5.50	12.7	1069	377
4	4a, 4b, 4c	5.50	13.4	944	1121
5	5a, 5b	5.50	13.1	446	1103
6	6a, 6b	3.50	9.9	584	370
7	7a, 7b	4.25	10.6	510	928
8	8a, 8b	4.50	11.7	656	769
9	9	4.00	11.4	651	395
10	10	3.25	6.4	550	775
11	11a, 11b	3.75	11.9	255	1434

11 Days: Option B

This itinerary is identical to Option A except for Days 10 and 11. It is useful for those who cannot get a booking at Rifugio Pian de Fontana as the evening of Day 10 is spent at Rifugio Bianchet instead. Option B's Day 10 is longer than that of Option A. Day 11 is therefore very short.

Day	Stages	Time (hr)	Km	Ascent (m)	Descent (m)
1	1	3.25	6.9	929	96
2	2a, 2b, 2c	4.75	13.1	613	880
3	3	5.50	12.7	1069	377
4	4a, 4b, 4c	5.50	13.4	944	1121
5	5a, 5b	5.50	13.1	446	1103
6	6a, 6b	3.50	9.9	584	370
7	7a, 7b	4.25	10.6	510	928
8	8a, 8b	4.50	11.7	656	769
9	9	4.00	11.4	651	395
10	10, 11a	5.25	12.2	805	1417
11	11b	1.75	6.1	0	792

10 Days

Days 6, 7 and 8 are longer and more challenging but your body and mind should be 'trail-hardened' by then.

Day	Stages	Time (hr)	Km	Ascent (m)	Descent (m)
1	1	3.25	6.9	929	96
2	2a, 2b, 2c	4.75	13.1	613	880
3	3	5.50	12.7	1069	377
4	4a, 4b, 4c	5.50	13.4	944	1121
5	5a, 5b	5.50	13.1	446	1103
6	6a, 6b, 7a	6.00	14.6	1019	687
7	7b, 8a	5.50	15.2	702	1118
8	8b, 9	4.75	13.8	680	657
9	10	3.25	6.4	550	775
10	11a, 11b	3.75	11.9	255	1434

9 Days

This schedule ramps things up a bit. The final day is the longest one with a knee-jerking 2209m of descent.

Day	Stages	Time (hr)	Km	Ascent (m)	Descent (m)
1	1	3.25	6.9	929	96
2	2a, 2b, 2c	4.75	13.1	613	880
3	3	5.50	12.7	1069	377
4	4a, 4b, 4c	5.50	13.4	944	1121
5	5a, 5b	5.50	13.1	446	1103
6	6a, 6b, 7a	6.00	14.6	1019	687
7	7b, 8a	5.50	15.2	702	1118
8	8b, 9	4.75	13.8	680	657
9	10, 11a, 11b	7.00	18.3	805	2209

8 Days

This itinerary toughens things up significantly. The first five days of the standard 11-day schedule are squeezed into four days. The first two days are challenging so you will want to arrive at the start in good physical condition.

Day	Stages	Time (hr)	Km	Ascent (m)	Descent (m)
1	1, 2a, 2b	6.00	14.8	982	928
2	2c, 3	7.50	17.9	1629	425
3	4a, 4b, 4c	5.50	13.4	944	1121
4	5a, 5b	5.50	13.1	446	1103
5	6a, 6b, 7a	6.00	14.6	1019	687
6	7b, 8a	5.50	15.2	702	1118
7	8b, 9	4.75	13.8	680	657
8	10, 11a, 11b	7.00	18.3	805	2209

AV1 Humour!

7 Days

For fit walkers used to trekking. You will need to be in good shape before starting. Every day is tough except for Day 6.

Day	Stages	Time (hr)	Km	Ascent (m)	Descent (m)
1	1, 2a, 2b	6.00	14.8	982	928
2	2c, 3	7.50	17.9	1629	425
3	4a, 4b, 4c, 5a	7.00	15.9	1004	1520
4	5b, 6a, 6b	7.50	20.5	970	1074
5	7a, 7b, 8a	8.00	19.9	1137	1435
6	8b, 9	4.75	13.8	680	657
7	10, 11a, 11b	7.00	18.3	805	2209

6 Days

These six relentless and challenging days are for very fit walkers only. It starts hard and stays hard all the way to the end.

Day	Stages	Time (hr)	Km	Ascent (m)	Descent (m)
1	1, 2a, 2b, 2c	8.00	20.0	1542	976
2	3, 4a	8.00	19.4	1167	1190
3	4b, 4c, 5a, 5b	8.50	19.8	1292	1411
4	6a, 6b, 7a, 7b	7.75	20.5	1094	1298
5	8a, 8b, 9	8.50	23.1	1307	1164
6	10, 11a, 11b	7.00	18.3	805	2209

Interesting geology on Stage 3

Variant Stages

Stage No	Start/Finish	Time (hr)	Km	Ascent (m)	Descent (m)	Max. Altitude (m)
v5	Rifugio Cinque Torri to Rifugio Città di Fiume (via Rifugio Croda da Lago)	4.75	13.6	645	864	2295
v6	Rifugio Città di Fiume to Rifugio Coldai (via Rifugio Venezia)	7.50	16.8	1320	1106	2476
v11	Rifugio Pian de Fontana to Bolzano Bellunese (Via Ferrata)	9.75	21.7	1187	2321	2372

Climbing through pastures on Stage 3

The path approaching Rifugio Pramperet (Stage 9)

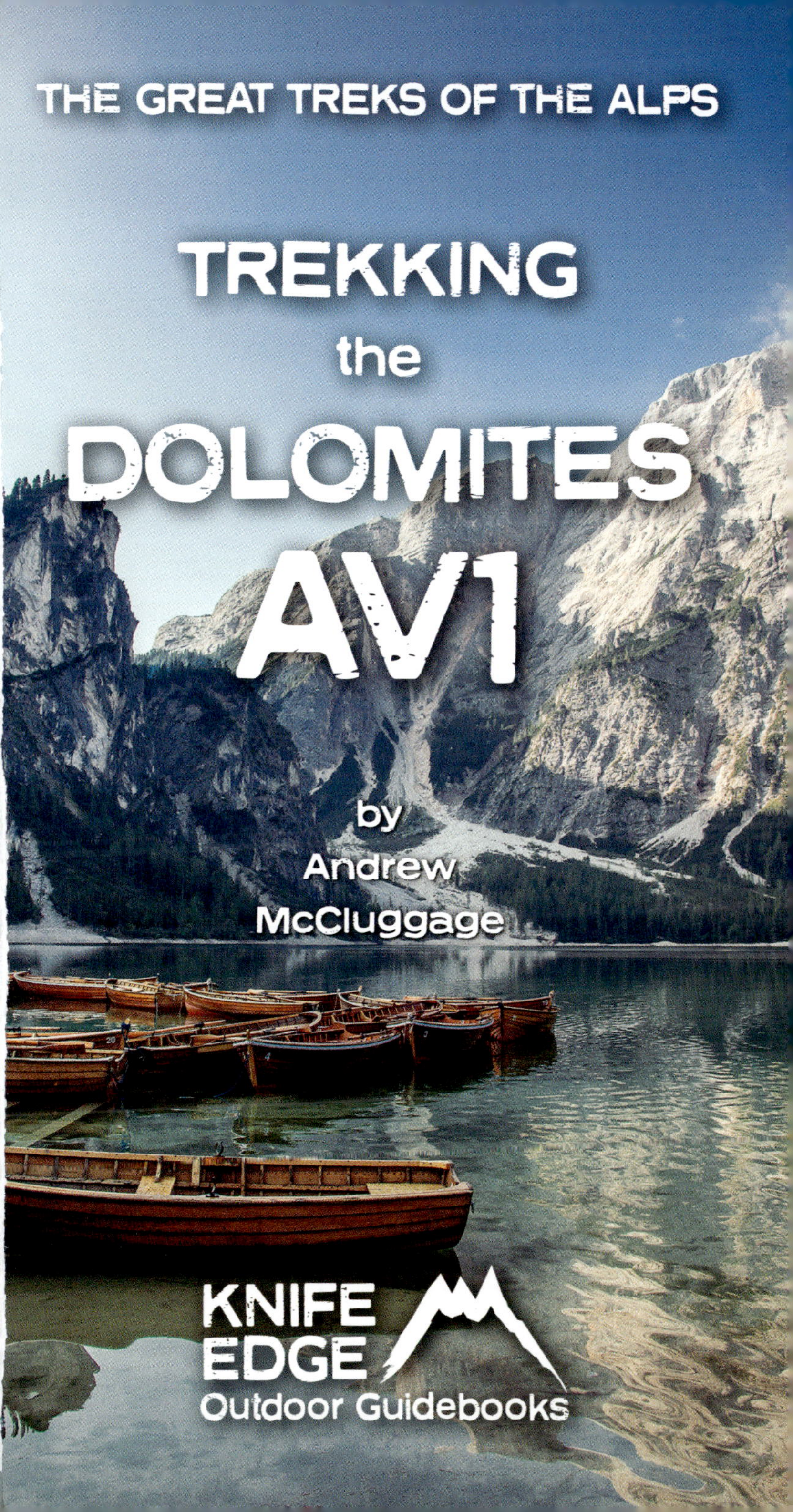
THE GREAT TREKS OF THE ALPS
TREKKING
the
DOLOMITES
AV1
by
Andrew
McCluggage
KNIFE
EDGE
Outdoor Guidebooks

About the Author

Andrew McCluggage is an outdoor writer and photographer from Northern Ireland. After 20 years as a corporate lawyer, he decided to do something interesting and started writing walking guidebooks.

His first book was Walking in the Briançonnais, a beautiful part of the French Alps. Since then, he has written a variety of guidebooks for hiking and trekking.

Other Knife Edge Outdoor Guidebooks written by Andrew include:

- Tour du Mont Blanc
- Trekking Iceland's Laugavegur Trail
- Walker's Haute Route: Chamonix to Zermatt
- Trekking the Corsica GR20
- Trekking the Mallorca GR221
- Tour of the Écrins National Park (GR54)
- Trekking the West Highland Way
- Trekking the Hadrian's Wall Path
- Trekking the Coast to Coast Path
- Trekking the Cotswold Way
- Trekking the South Downs Way
- Walking Chamonix-Mont Blanc
- Walking Brittany
- Northern Ireland: the Unmissable Walks
- The Mourne Mountains
- Big Hikes in the Mourne Mountains

Accommodation

Cutting the grass at Rifugio Pian de Fontana

The AV1 is a popular trek and the quality of accommodation has improved greatly in recent years. You will stay in mountain huts ('rifugi') which offer dormitory accommodation, meals and alcohol. Sometimes private rooms are also available but they book up very quickly. The huts are situated in the heart of the mountains where they are normally accessible only to walkers. A stay in a rifugio can be one of the highlights of a mountain adventure such as the AV1. They are basic but they are good value: a bed, dinner and breakfast should cost around €50-65.

To stay in a rifugio, you will need a sleeping sheet which is a thin bag made of silk or cotton. They can be purchased cheaply at most outdoor shops in the UK, US or Europe. The huts provide blankets/duvet and a pillow. Most of the huts on the AV1 still charge for showers. The huts are normally manned from mid-June to the end of September. If you are a member of a mountaineering association in your home country, bring your membership card as many rifugi offer discounts to association members.

Our Favourite Places to Stay

1. Rifugio Pian de Fontana (Stage 10)
2. Rifugio Fanes (Stage 2c)
3. Rifugio Cinque Torri (Stage 4b)
4. Rifugio Pramperet (Stage 9)
5. Rifugio Passo Staulanza (Stage 6a)

In July and August, forward booking is essential: these days, most people have their entire trip booked before they depart. During those months, the days of 'winging it' are gone. Even outside of July and August, it is wise to book ahead, particularly at weekends and on sub-stages where there is only one place to stay. In June and September, fewer people walk the route so there is less demand for accommodation. However, the number of AV1 trekkers in June and September is increasing each year. In these periods, you can sometimes still get away with only booking a day or two in advance but you might be unlucky and end up without anywhere to stay: for example, you can get caught out if a large group has booked up a lot of beds. In early June and towards the end of September, some accommodation may be closed so check in advance.

Unless you are using a tour company, you will need to book each of the huts separately: there is no central booking website for the AV1. This can be a time-consuming, and sometimes frustrating, process. Some huts have an online booking system which is easy to use. However, with other huts you will need to send an email requesting your dates: response times vary and are sometimes frustratingly slow. You could also try calling the huts: not all of the staff speak English but the situation has certainly improved in recent years. Many huts insist upon non-refundable deposits to secure reservations (€15-20 per person). See below for some booking tips.

'Hot-spots' where accommodation can be particularly hard to secure

- **Rifugio Biella (Stage 1):** it is the first stop on the AV1 and comes after a long climb so it is a popular stopping point.
- **Rifugio Fanes (Stage 2c):** a modern and clean hut with great food. It books up fast.
- **Rifugio Lagazuoi (Stage 3):** it is situated at the top of a cable car so it is always busy.
- **Rifugio Averau (Stage 4c):** the food at this small hut is so good that it is almost always full. Its location, close to Cortina, means that it also attracts day-walkers.
- **Rifugio Città di Fiume (Stage 5b/V5):** this small hut fills up quickly, maybe because the subsequent one, Rifugio Staulanza, is more expensive.
- **Rifugio Pian de Fontana (Stage 10):** this hut is small and there is nowhere else to stay so book ahead.

Full accommodation listings are provided below. All contact details were correct at the date of press but be aware that this information frequently changes. Please let us know about any changes.

Belluno makes a great place to celebrate the completion of the AV1

AV1 Booking Tips

- The AV1 becomes more popular each year. To ensure that you secure your accommodation of choice, book as early as you can. Many trekkers start booking in October for the following summer.
- When emailing huts, it can be advantageous to write in Italian using Google Translate or another equivalent translation service. Many maintain that emails in Italian are answered more quickly than those in English.
- Try to book 'hot-spots' first (see page 20). Once you have secured the accommodation which books up most quickly, you can normally slot in the rest of your accommodation more easily. If you leave hot-spots until last then you might have to unwind and rebook other reservations if any hot-spots that you desire are unavailable.
- Watch out for weekends (even in low season). This is when many locals come out to play and huts are often full to capacity.
- Private rooms usually book up very quickly.

Rifugio Biella

A typical dormitory

Hut Etiquette

Take off your boots before entering

Tell the gardien (hut manager) that you have arrived

Always use a sleeping sheet

Pay before you go to bed

Do not make noise after 9pm as most walkers go to bed early

If you change your plans, always call to cancel your reservation to allow someone else to take your place

Camping

One of the steep gullies crossed on Stage 9

Although some people do it, camping on the AV1 can be a challenge for the following reasons:

- **Campsites:** there are none on the main route so you would have to camp wild or leave the route.
- **Food Supply:** there are no shops on the main route of the AV1 so you would have to exit the trek to buy food (see 'Escape Routes' below).
- **Pack Weight:** physically, camping is a tougher option as you need to carry more gear (tent, sleeping bag, sleeping mat, cooker, food, etc). The extra weight makes a difference to your legs over 121km. That said, some incredibly lightweight camping gear is available these days.
- **Wild Camping Rules:** the rules governing wild camping in Italy are difficult to ascertain because there is no single national regulation. Rather, the rules are implemented regionally: in the regions of the AV1, wild camping seems to be permitted for a period of 24hr in places where no specific prohibitions have been put in place by the relevant local authorities. However, there are specific prohibitions in place in the regional parks crossed on the AV1. This means that wild camping is prohibited on much of the territory crossed on Stages 1-4 and 9-11.

Rules and laws are subject to change so check with the local tourist offices before setting out. If you get caught breaking the rules, you could face a stiff fine: we warned you!

You do hear of AV1 trekkers who wild camp by being discrete, staying high and only pitching-up late in the day. But we cannot condone the breaking of rules. If you do camp wild, always take your rubbish with you (including toilet paper) and bury your toilet waste away from watercourses. Leave no trace.

Accommodation Listings

An AV1 marker at Forcella del Moschesin (Stage 9)

PRs: Private Rooms

Stage No.	Accommodation	Facilities	Opening Dates	Contact Details
Lago di Braies	Hotel Lago di Braies	PRs	All year	+39 0474 748602 hotel@pragserwildsee.com www.lagodibraies.com
1	Rifugio Biella	46 beds	late June to end Sept	+39 335 1431251 info@rifugiobiella.com www.rifugiobiella.com
2a	Rifugio Sennes	60 beds PRs	June to early Oct	+39 0474 646355 +39 328 7945579 info@sennes.com www.sennes.com
2b Off-route	Rifugio Fodara Vedla	36 beds PRs	June to Oct	+39 348 8537471 rifugio@fodara.it www.fodara.it
2b	Rifugio Pederü	30 beds PRs	June to mid-Oct	+39 0474 834316 info@pederue.it www.pederue.it
2c	Ücia dles Muntagnoles	4 rooms B&B only	mid-June to early Oct	+39 347 5214753 www.muntagnoles.com
2c	Rifugio Fanes	70 beds PRs	June to mid-Oct	+39 0474 453001 +39 0474 501097 info@rifugiofanes.com www.rifugiofanes.com
2c Off-route	Rifugio Lavarella	51 beds PRs Micro-brewery	mid-June to mid-Oct	+39 0474 501094 +39 0474 501079 rifugio@lavarella.it www.lavarella.it
3	Ütia de Gran Fanes	12 beds	Variable	+39 346 2193374 +39 349 3172061 Difficult to contact

Stage No.	Accommodation	Facilities	Opening Dates	Contact Details
3 Rifugio Scotoni Detour	Camping Saas Dlacia (1.3km off-route from 5)	Camping	June to mid-Oct	+39 0471 849527 info@sassdlacia.com www.campingsassdlacia.it
3 Rifugio Scotoni Detour	Rifugio Scotoni	21 beds PRs	June to Sept	+39 0471 847330 info@scotoni.it www.scotoni.it
3	Rifugio Lagazuoi	76 beds PRs	June to Sept	+39 0436 867303 +39 340 7195306 info@rifugiolagazuoi.com www.rifugiolagazuoi.com
4a	Rifugio Dibona	65 beds	mid-June to end Sept	+39 0436 860294 +39 333 1434408 www.rifugiodibona.business.site
4b	Rifugio Cinque Torri	24 beds PRs	June to Sept	+39 0436 2902/2863 +39 0436 866853 info@rifugio5torri.it www.cortinadelicious.it
4c	Rifugio Scoiattoli	42 beds PRs	mid-June to end-Sept	+39 0436 867939 +39 333 8146960 info@rifugioscoittoli.it www.rifugioscoiattoli.it
4c	Rifugio Averau	22 beds PRs	mid-June to Sept	+39 0436 4660 +39 335 6868066 rifugioaverau@gmail.com www.rifugioaverau.it
4c	Rifugio Nuvolau	24 beds	mid-June to late Sept	+39 0436 867938 info@rifugionuvolau.it www.rifugionuvolau.it
5a	Berghotel Passo Giau	12 beds PRs	June to mid-Oct	+39 346 0696745 info@passogiau.it www.passogiau.it
5b/v5	Rifugio Città di Fiume	25 beds	mid-June to late Sept	+39 320 0377432 info@rifugiocittadifiume.it www.rifugiocittadifiume.it
v5	Rifugio Croda da Lago	51 beds	June to Nov	+39 0436 862085 info@crodadalago.it www.crodadalago.it
6a	Rifugio Passo Staulanza	50 beds PRs	Mid-June to end Sept	+39 338 7900120 +39 0437 788709 info@staulanza.it www.staulanza.it
6b/v6	Rifugio Coldai	88 beds	mid-June to late Sept	+39 0437 789160 infocoldai@gmail.com www.rifugiocoldai.com
v6	Rifugio Venezia	62 beds	mid-June to mid-Sept	+39 0436 9684 +39 320 0103872 rifugio.venezia@libero.it www.rifugiovenezia.it

Stage No.	Accommodation	Facilities	Opening Dates	Contact Details
v6	Rifugio Palafavera	25 beds PRs	mid-June to mid-Sept	+39 0437 789133 info@palafavera.com www.palafavera.com
v6	Rifugio Monte Pelmo	8 beds	June to Sept	+39 0437 789359
v6	Camping Palafavera	Camping; Grocery shop	June to Sept	+39 0437 788506 palafavera@sunrise.it www.campingpalafavera.com
7a	Rifugio Tissi	65 beds	mid-June to Sept	+39 0437 721644 +39 347 5931833 rifugio.tissi@gmail.com www.rifugiotissi.com
7b	Rifugio Vazzoler	52 beds	mid-June to Sept	+39 0437 1956619 +39 0437 660008 rifugiovazzoler@gmail.com www.rifugiovazzoler.com
8a	Rifugio Carestiato	30 beds	June to Sept	+39 0437 62949 info@rifugiocarestiato.com www.rifugiocarestiato.com
8a	Rifugio Capanna Trieste (2km off-route from 1)	18 beds PRs	April to Oct	+39 0437 660122 +39 340 5028699 rifugiocapannatrieste@gmail.com www.rifugiocapannatrieste.it
8b	Rifugio Passo Duran	25 beds PRs Laundry facilities	mid-June to end Sept	+39 349 6848307 info@rifugiopassoduran.it www.rifugiopassoduran.it
8b	Rifugio S. Sebastiano	25 beds PRs	mid-June to end Sept	+39 0437 62360 +39 328 1630580 info@passoduran.it www.passoduran.it
9	Rifugio Pramperet	25 beds	mid-June to mid-Sept	+39 0437 1956153 info@rifugiosommarivaalpramperet.it www.rifugiosommarivaalpramperet.it
9 Forno di Zoldo Escape Route	Camping Al Pez (8km off-route from 5)	Camping	All year	+39 0437 787576 alpez@sunrise.it www.campingalpez.com
10	Rifugio Pian de Fontana	33 beds	mid-June to end Sept	+39 335 6096819 +39 0437 1956135 piandefontana@livecom.it www.piandefontana.it
11a	Rifugio Bianchet	40 beds	June to Sept	+39 0437 669226 +39 335 6446975 rifugiobianchet@hotmail.com www.caiveneto.it

Stage No.	Accommodation	Facilities	Opening Dates	Contact Details
v11	Rifugio 7° Alpini	60 beds	mid-June to mid-Sept	+39 0437 941631 +39 348 5417793 infosettimoalpini@gmail.com www.rifugiosettimoalpini.it
Belluno	Albergo Cappello e Cadore	32 rooms	All year	+39 0437 940246 info@albergocappello.com www.albergocappello.com
Belluno	Albergo delle Alpi	40 rooms	All year	+39 0437 940545 +39 0437 940565 info@dellealpi.it www.dellealpi.it
Belluno	Casa per Ferie	59 rooms	All year	+39 0437 944460 casaferie@diocesi.it www.casaferie.diocesi.it
Belluno	Albergo al Ponte della Vittoria	10 rooms	All year	+39 0437 925270 info@alpontedellavittoria.it www.alpontedellavittoria.it
Belluno	Hotel Europa	-	All year	+39 0437 930196 europabelluno@gmail.com www.europabelluno.it
Belluno	Hotel Astor	18 Rooms	All year	+39 0437 943756 hotel@astorbelluno.it www.astorbelluno.it
Belluno	Casa Zavi B&B	3 Rooms	All year	+39 329 7939686 www.casazavi.it

Rifugio Biella (Stage 1)

Food

Fruit and vegetables on sale in Belluno

As Italy has arguably the best food in the world, it is no surprise that the AV1 delivers probably the finest culinary experience of any trek in the world. However, there is not just Italian cuisine on offer: in the German speaking parts of the Dolomites (closest to the Austrian border), the food is predominantly Austrian. Many huts offer both types of food but it is noticeable, as you proceed S, that the emphasis changes from Austrian to Italian.

Italian menus are typically divided into 4 courses:

- **Antipasto:** a starter which is usually cold. Cheeses and cold meats are common.
- **Primo piatto:** the 'first' course, which is hot. Normally this will be polenta (which is made from cornmeal), soup, pasta or risotto (rice). Pasta is commonly served with a meat sauce ('al ragù') or a tomato sauce ('al pomodoro'). The soup is often 'minestrone' which is made with thickly-cut vegetables.
- **Secondo:** the 'second' course which is normally meat such as pork ('maiale'), beef ('manzo') or veal ('vitello').
- **Dolce:** the dessert. Coffee-based Tiramisu (which means 'pick me up') will need little introduction. Panna Cotta, a cream based dessert, is also common.

Italian food is so popular around the world that most will be familiar with the basics but Austrian food is less well-known. Knödels ('Canederli' in Italian) are on most menus in the Dolomites: they are bread dumplings served in a variety of ways, sometimes with a meat stew ('Gulasch') and sometimes in a soup ('Canederli in Brodo'). For dessert, Apfelstrudel (a delicious type of apple pie) is served almost everywhere but, as everyone seems to have their own secret recipe, it differs from hut to hut.

Walkers are hungry people and most huts cater for this providing breakfast, dinner and packed lunches for the following day. In huts, the evening meal is generally three courses: primo, secondo and dolce. In some huts, there is a set menu which normally gives you the choice of two or three options for each course. In other huts, evening meals are 'à la carte' so you can order whatever you want from a menu. Vegetarian and vegan options will normally be available on request.

Breakfast varies in quality: in rifugi which are off the beaten track, it is often the functional minimum of coffee, bread and jam, perhaps with some cheeses or cold meats if you are lucky. Closer to civilisation, quality tends to improve.

There are no shops on the AV1 so, once your initial food supplies are exhausted, you will need to buy packed lunches from the huts (before leaving in the morning) or stop at another hut for a meal at lunchtime. Huts are well spaced so you will normally find one every few hours but you should plan ahead to ensure that you know where your next food stop will be. If you want a packed lunch then order it the night before: they cost around €10.

Our Favourite Places to Eat

1. Rifugio Cinque Torri (Stage 4b)
2. Rifugio Averau (Stage 4c)
3. Rifugio Passo Staulanza (Stage 6a)
4. Rifugio Fanes (Stage 2c)
5. Rifugio Coldai (Stage 6b)

Rabbit

Salads are widely available

Spaghetti al ragù

Pork chop

Pizza Diavola

Walnut cake

Travel

The rocky trail to Rifugio Carestiato (Stage 8a)

Getting to the Staging Points

Venice Airport is probably the best place to fly into as there are regular buses from the airport to Cortina d'Ampezzo (one of the Staging Points). In summer, it is wise to book the bus online in advance: Cortina Express (www.cortinaexpress.it), ATVO (www.atvo.it) and Flixbus (www.flixbus.com) all run this service which takes around 2.5hr.

The airports at Verona, Milan and Bergamo can also be used. From Verona, you can travel by train to Villabassa/Niederdorf and Dobbiaco/Toblach (3-4hr including a change at Fortezza/Franzensfeste). From Milan and Bergamo, you will first need to travel to Verona by bus or train. Timetables can be found at www.trenitalia.com. Trenitalia also has an excellent smartphone app in English enabling you to book train tickets in advance.

Munich airport is another option as there are trains from Munich to Villabassa/Niederdorf and Dobbiaco/Toblach (see www.bahn.de). The trains take 5-6hr with a change at Fortezza/Franzensfeste.

Alternatively, you could leave a car at the car parks at Lago di Braies (which are fairly expensive) and use public transport to return to it at the end of the trek. This would involve a long train ride from Belluno to Villabassa and then the bus to Lago di Braies (see below).

Staging Point	Travel to Staging Point
Villabassa/ Niederdorf	**Option 1:** Train from Verona, Milan, Bergamo or Munich **Option 2:** Bus to Cortina d'Ampezzo from Venice Mestre/Venice Airport. Then bus 445 from Cortina d'Ampezzo to Dobbiaco and bus 442 from Dobbiaco to Villabassa. See **www.sad.it**
Dobbiaco/ Toblach	**Option 1:** Train from Verona, Milan, Bergamo or Munich **Option 2:** Bus to Cortina d'Ampezzo from Venice Mestre/Venice Airport. Then bus 445 from Cortina d'Ampezzo. See **www.sad.it**
Cortina d'Ampezzo	Bus from Venice Mestre or Venice Airport

Getting from the Staging Points to the Trail-head (at Lago di Braies/Pragser Wildsee)

Staging Point	Travel to Trail-head
Villabassa/ Niederdorf	Bus 442: in summer this runs twice every hour starting at around 8am. It takes 20min. In peak season, this bus must be booked in advance: see **www.prags.bz** or **www.sad.it**
Dobbiaco/ Toblach	Bus 442: in summer this runs twice every hour starting at around 8am. It takes 30min. In peak season, this bus must be booked in advance: see **www.prags.bz** or **www.sad.it**
Cortina d'Ampezzo	Bus 445 to Dobbiaco/Toblach and then Bus 442 to Lago di Braies. During the summer, Bus 445 runs every few hours, from around 8am: you can pay onboard (without advance booking). It is usually timed to connect with Bus 442 (see above). From Cortina, the earliest you can reach Lago di Braies is 9:30am. See **www.sad.it**

Getting away from Belluno

There are regular trains from Belluno to Venice Mestre (which is a short bus ride from Venice Airport). There are also trains to Verona which has train and bus connections to Milan, Bergamo and Munich. There are also bus services to Venice and elsewhere which depart from Belluno train station.

The descent to Rifugio Vazzoler (Stage 7b)

On the Trail

Each path in the Dolomites is numbered so navigation is normally straightforward

Costs

As vacations go, long-distance walking in Europe is relatively inexpensive. The walking itself is free as no permits are required. In rifugi, breakfast, dinner and a dormitory bed normally cost around €55-70. Private rooms cost a bit more per person. Packed lunches cost around €10. If you camp and cook for yourself, then you could get by on much less.

Weather

The Dolomites have a relatively dry and predictable climate compared to mountains in the UK. However, conditions can still change quickly so be prepared for rain. Furthermore, snow is always possible on mountain passes and summits, even in the middle of summer. Mountains can be dangerous so treat them with respect and caution, even if the weather forecast is favourable.

The region has a number of micro-climates with the weather often differing from valley to valley. It is possible therefore to find blazing sunshine on one side of a pass and cloud or rain over the other side.

Meteo.it provides national, regional and local forecasts at www.meteo.it. It also provides, free of charge, an excellent smartphone app with regularly updated local forecasts. Local forecasts are also displayed at tourist information offices and rifugi. Or ask the rifugio managers whose local knowledge of weather (and indeed other matters) is often invaluable.

Maps

In this book, we have included the best maps available. Each sub-stage has its own 1:25,000 scale map produced by Tabacco. Occasionally, a map has been reduced slightly to fit on the page. Although these maps are normally sufficient for navigation, a sheet map can be helpful, particularly in bad weather. Also, with a sheet map you get a better feel for the geography of the region as it helps you to identify peaks and landmarks sighted along the way.

We like the detail on the sheet maps made by Tabacco: three 1:25,000 sheets would be needed to cover the main AV1: 031 Dolomiti di Braies, 03 Cortina d'Ampezzo and 025 Dolomiti di Zoldo. The Stage v11 variant is covered by sheet 024 Prealpi e Dolomiti Bellunesi. Alternatively, Tappeiner's map 167 Dolomiten-Höhenweg covers the entire AV1 on one 1:25,000 sheet: it is not as detailed as the Tabacco maps but the AV1 is clearly marked on it in yellow.

However, perhaps the best overall solution is to combine this book with a smart phone app. Tabacco's app covers the entire AV1: you buy and download the specific map tiles that you wish to use: the tiles you need are 001E, 001F, 001G, 001H, 001I, E02E, E02F, E02G, E02H, E02I and E02J.

Paths and Waymarking

Much of the AV1 uses clear paths which are easy to follow. Each path in the Dolomites has its own specific number: these numbers are indicated clearly on the maps and we have also listed the relevant numbers in the introduction for each sub-stage. Furthermore, on the trail, there are frequent waymarks (painted on trees and rocks) and signs which display the path numbers. Consequently, navigation in good conditions is generally straightforward. As a general rule of thumb, keep on a path unless told otherwise. Bear in mind though that waymarking varies in quality and is at the mercy of the environment: markings can fade or be obscured by rockfalls or landslides.

Although you mainly follow well-defined tracks and paths, there are some short sections of the route which are more challenging. Some parts of the AV1 are quite exposed. Furthermore, occasionally the trail disappears over rocks and boulders: navigation there can be more difficult (particularly in bad conditions) and you must concentrate on following the waymarks. Also, you should watch your footing carefully when walking over the rocks and boulders.

Some of the most challenging sections of the main AV1 are listed below. You can bypass each of them using the alternative directions provided in the walk descriptions.

- **Stage 3:** immediately after Forcela dl Lêch, the path zigzags steeply downwards though a precipitous gully. Watch your footing on the unstable surface.
- **Stage 4a:** after Forcella Col dei Bòs, there is a short but delicate traverse underneath Tofana de Rozes. Occasionally, parts of the exposed path are destroyed by rock-fall.
- **Stage 5a:** shortly after leaving Rifugio Nuvolau, there are two steep and exposed sections where cables have been bolted into the rock to assist you. This section is best avoided if you have a fear of heights.

- **Stage 10:** the wildest and hardest section of the AV1 with a steep climb, an exposed knife-edge ridge and a knee-jerking descent. This section is best avoided if you have a fear of heights.

If you see mountain biking signs, then take care: mountain bikes are fast and often quiet. A collision between a walker and a mountain bike could be serious.

Water

Drinking water in the Dolomites is the subject of regular debate. Except in very dry seasons or towards the end of September, water is usually plentiful in rivers and streams. Water is also available at rifugi (except Rifugio Tissi). Many walkers regularly drink untreated water from these sources without any issues. However, others insist upon filtering or treating the water first to minimise the risk of contaminants. You will have to weigh up the risks and make up your own mind. If, like many, you do decide to drink the water untreated, there are a few rules that you should follow to reduce any risk:

- Avoid water where there is evidence nearby of animals, especially cows or sheep: carcasses (of dead animals) or faeces can cause contamination
- Do not collect water downstream from buildings or grazing areas
- Only drink from moving water. The faster the better
- The bigger the river/stream the better
- Generally the higher the altitude the better

If you do wish to treat your water, this can be done by way of portable filters, steripens or purification chemicals. The effectiveness of the different products and methods varies and is beyond the scope of this book so do your research before your trip.

Also remember that the availability of water in streams may vary depending upon the season: generally water-courses are fullest in June and decline throughout the walking season. It is good practice to fill your water bottles each day before leaving your accommodation. Start with at least 1.5 litres per person.

Escape Routes

The AV1 has many exit points with road access, enabling a walker to leave the route early, but the availability of public transport at these locations varies (see route descriptions). The key exit points include: Rifugio Pederü (Stage 2b), Passo Falzàrego (near Rifugio Lagazuoi; Stage 3), Rifugio Scoiattoli (Stage 4c), Passo Giau (Stage 5a), Passo Staulanza (Stage 6a), Passo Duran (Stage 8b; no public transport) and Malga di Pramperet (off the route of Stage 9). During stages, escape is difficult and normally, once started, you are committed.

Often cable-ways are used to supply the rifugi

What to Take

The magnificent path to Forcela dl Lèch (Stage 3)

When undertaking a long-distance route in the Dolomites, you should be properly equipped for the worst terrain and the worst weather conditions which you could encounter: rain, cold and possibly snow. Being cold and wet at high altitude is unpleasant and can be dangerous. However, the dilemma is that you should also consider weight and avoid carrying anything unnecessary. The heavier your pack, the harder the climbs will be. It is perfectly possible to get by with a pack weighing 5-6kg (excluding water) yet most hikers' packs weigh much more. Be ruthless as every ounce counts. Fortunately, modern equipment helps with this dilemma: there is some fantastic light-weight kit available now.

Layering of clothing is the key to warmth. Do not wear cotton: it does not dry quickly and gets cold. Modern walking clothes are light so make sure that you have a spare set to change into if you get wet.

Recommended Basic Kit ☑

Boots/Shoes	Good quality, properly fitting and worn in. Some hike in trail-running shoes but others prefer light boots with ankle support.	
Socks	3 pairs of good quality, quick drying walking socks: wash one, wear one, spare one. Wash them regularly and change them daily, helping to avoid blisters.	
Waterproof jacket and trousers	Waterproof and breathable. Some people do not bother with waterproof trousers but we like to carry light ones just in case.	
Base layers	3 T-shirts and pants of man-made fabrics or merino wool, which wick moisture away from your body: wash one, wear one, spare one.	
Fleeces	2 fleeces. Man–made fabrics. Wear one, spare one.	

Shorts/ Trousers	2 pairs of walking trousers. Wear one, spare one. Convertible ones are practical as you can remove the legs on warm days.	
Warm hat and gloves	Even in summer it can be cold at altitude, especially in the evening and early morning.	
Down jacket	Even in summer it can be cold at altitude, especially in the evening and early morning.	
Rucksack	Get a light one. 35-45 litres should be sufficient unless you are camping. Well-padded shoulder straps and waist band. Much of the weight of the pack should sit on your hips rather than your shoulders.	
Waterproof pack liner	Rucksacks are not very waterproof. A liner will keep your gear dry if it rains.	
Whistle	For emergencies. Many rucksacks have one incorporated into the sternum strap.	
Head-torch with spare batteries	It is good practice to carry a head-torch for emergencies. This can help you if you get caught out late and enables you to signal to rescuers.	
Basic first aid kit	Including plasters, a bandage and antiseptic wipes.	
Map and compass	For maps see above. A GPS unit or a smartphone app can be a useful addition but they are no substitute for a map and compass: after all, batteries can run out and electronics can fail.	
Knife	Such as a Swiss army knife. You are going to need to cut that cheese!	
Sunglasses, sun hat, sunscreen and lip salve	The sun in Italy is strong so do not set out without these items.	
Walking poles	These transfer weight from your legs onto your arms, keeping you fresher. They also save your knees (particularly on descents) and can reduce the likelihood of falling or twisting an ankle.	
Phone and charger (with EU adapter)	A smartphone is a very useful tool on a trek. It can be used for emergencies. Furthermore, apps for weather, mapping and hotel booking are invaluable. It can also replace your camera to save weight.	
Towel	Lightweight trekking towel. Rifugi do not provide towels.	
Shower gel	A small hotel-size bottle should be enough to last the trek, saving a lot of weight.	

Ziplock plastic bag	A lightweight way of keeping money, passport and credit cards dry.
Sleeping sheet	A thin bag made of silk or cotton. Required to sleep in refuges.
Ear plugs	You will thank us when someone in your dormitory snores.
Space blanket or emergency bag	Very light but it could save your life.
Food	Carry some emergency food over and above your planned daily ration. Energy bars, nuts and dried fruit are all good.
Water	Start each day with at least 1.5 litres of water per person. Hydration packs with tubes facilitate more effective hydration by enabling drinking on the move. Bring a filter or purification tablets if required.

Baggage Transfer

On some treks, you can use baggage transfer services to transport your bags to your accommodation each night so that you only need to carry a small day-pack on the trail. However, due to the remote location of many huts, baggage transfer is only possible at certain locations on the AV1 (which have road access): usually, Rifugio Pederu, Rifugio Staulanza, Passo Duran and sometimes, Passo Giau and Rifugio Cinque Torre. These locations are not on consecutive nights for most trekkers so you will need to carry your own gear anyway for the other overnight stops: however, baggage transfer does enable you to swap out your clothes every few days and to pack some luxuries. Most companies offering unguided tours can arrange for your baggage to be dropped off at these locations.

You could also use baggage transfer services to transfer your surplus baggage (that you will not be carrying on the trail) between your accommodation at your start and finish points. This is not cheap but it would save you the hassle of having to return to your start point to pick it up.

The following businesses can organise baggage transfers:

- **DC Transfers:** www.dctransfers.it; booking@dctransfers.it
- **Dolomiti Transfer:** www.dolomititransfer.net; info@dolomititransfer.net; +39 389 5114060
- **Claudio Bus:** www.claudiobus.eu; info@claudiobus.eu; +39 0471 847033
- **Cortina Car Service:** www.taxicortina.it; info@taxicortina.it; +39 338 6611510
- **Taxi Alleghe:** www.taxialleghe.com; info@taxialleghe.com; +39 340 6796016

Safety

Classic Dolomite scenery on Stage 9

On a calm summer's day the Dolomites are paradise. But a sudden weather shift or an injury can change things dramatically so treat the mountains with respect and be conscious of your experience levels and physical capabilities. The following is a non-exhaustive list of recommendations:

- The fitter you are at the start of your trip, the more you will enjoy the walking
- Before you set out each day, study the route and make plans based upon the abilities of the weakest member of your party
- Get a weather forecast (daily if possible) and reassess your plans in light of it. Avoid exposed routes if the weather is uncertain
- Start early to avoid ascending during the hottest part of the day and to allow more surplus time in case something goes wrong
- Bring a map and compass and know how to use them
- It can be sensible to call ahead to your accommodation and tell them what time you will arrive. If you do not turn up then they can raise the alarm
- Carry surplus food and clothing for emergencies
- Never be too proud to turn back if you find the going too tough or if the weather deteriorates
- Do not stray from the route so as to avoid getting lost and to help prevent erosion of the landscape
- Avoid exposed high ground in a thunderstorm. If you get caught out in one then drop your walking poles and stay away from trees, overhanging rocks, metal structures and caves. Generally accepted advice is to squat on your pack and keep as low as possible
- In the event of an accident, move an injured person into a safe place and administer any necessary first aid. Keep the victim warm. Establish your exact coordinates and, if possible, use your cell-phone to call for help. The emergency numbers are set out on page 1. If you have no signal then send someone for help
- Mountain biking is popular in the Dolomites so watch out. A collision with a bike would not be pleasant

General Information

Enjoying the views at Portèla dei Pezedèi (Stage 10)

Language: In some parts of the Dolomites (normally those near to the Austrian border), German is widely spoken. Elsewhere, Italian is the main language. The ancient language of Ladin is also still spoken by some inhabitants but you are unlikely to hear it. These days, many locals working in the huts will have some basic English at least. On the trail, it is good manners to make an effort to say 'hello' in German or Italian. If you do so, then you will get a much more positive and friendly response from locals.

Charging electronic devices: You can charge devices at most huts. Continental 2-pin plugs are used so visitors from outside Continental Europe will need an adapter.

Money: Italy uses the Euro(€). There are ATMs in Villabassa, Dobbiaco and Cortina d'Ampezzo. However, on the route itself there are none so make sure that you have enough cash before you start. It is prudent not to leave money withdrawals until the last minute in case an ATM is out of order. Most (but not all) of the huts now accept credit cards but it is wise to carry cash too, in case credit card machines are out of order.

Visas: Citizens of the European Union do not need a visa to visit Italy. At the time of writing, citizens of the UK, Australia, New Zealand, Canada and the US do not need a visa for stays of up to three months.

Cell-phones: Cell-phone reception is sporadic on the AV1 so do not rely on it completely. When you have network, 3G/4G services are widely available so access to the internet from smartphones is normally possible.

International dialling codes: The country code for Italy is +39. If dialling from overseas, the 0 in Italian area codes is not omitted.

Wifi: Most huts on the AV1 now have wifi.

Insurance: Mountain rescue services may not be free and therefore it is wise to have adequate insurance which covers hiking. Visitors from the UK/EU should also make sure that they have the free Global Health Insurance Card (GHIC)/European Health Insurance Card (EHIC) but remember that often this will only cover part of your medical treatment so insurance is still recommended. Also, the GHIC/EHIC will not cover the rescue itself.

Emergencies: The emergency telephone numbers are 112 and 118.

Ticks: As is often the case in Europe, ticks are present on sections of the AV1, particularly wooded areas towards the S of the route. They can carry Lyme disease or tick-borne encephalitis so check yourself regularly. Remove ticks with tweezers (making sure you get all of it out) and then disinfect the area.

The path to Rifugio Pramperet (Stage 9)

Wildlife

A young Ibex

Early morning is the best time for seeing wildlife and the first party on the trail has the best chance of a sighting.

Ibex: A member of the goat family with long scimitar-shaped horns. It was saved from extinction by the Savoy kings who banned most hunting in 1821 and created a royal reserve in 1856 (which finally became Italy's Gran Paradiso National Park). After a series of reintroductions in the 20th century, they are now present again in the Dolomites.

Chamois: Another type of mountain goat which is smaller than the ibex and is widespread in the regions of the AV1. It has shorter horns which do not have deep ridges. Chamois are frequently spotted in herds. They are much more wary of humans than ibex.

Deer: Various species are common below the tree-line. Look out for them in forests early in the morning.

Marmots: Everyone loves these fat rodents which are easily spotted in summer when they graze relentlessly to put on layers of fat to last the long winter hibernation. They live in colonies in grassy parts of the mountains, often standing upright on their hind legs like a meerkat. They whistle as you approach to warn their colony of an intruder.

Wild Boar: A member of the pig family with small tusks. They are common in forests but hard to spot. In the unlikely event that you see one, keep your distance because they can be dangerous.

Marmots are plentiful!

Bears and Wolves: Previously hunted to extinction in Italy, reintroductions and other conservation efforts in recent decades have increased their numbers. They are protected but their presence is controversial. Wolves are particularly unpopular with shepherds who lose many sheep to them.

Other mammals: Squirrels, foxes, badgers and mice are fairly common below the tree-line.

Fish: species of trout are found in rivers, streams and lakes.

Ptarmigan: A grouse-like bird. Its plumage is white in the winter and largely brown in the summer.

Golden Eagle (pictured left): During the hot parts of the day, they can sometimes be seen circling in the thermals to gain altitude as they scan the ground for prey.

Reptiles/Amphibians: there are some snakes including vipers and adders (which are both venomous): if you spot one, keep your distance. There are also lizards, slow worms, frogs and salamanders.

The high pastures on Stage 3

Flowers

Doronico or Leopard's Bane

The Dolomites are home to thousands of plant species including the incredible wild-flowers. June is a fabulous month for flowers, which wait patiently throughout the winter for the snow to clear and then rapidly spring to life. At this time, carpets of different colours cover the slopes and pastures. Although spring is the peak time for flowers, there are still plenty throughout the summer. Look out for the following:

Alpenrose: A bright pink member of the Rhododendron family which coats the slopes at altitude in June/July.

Edelweiss: Probably the most famous alpine plant, perhaps because it has a song named after it. This rare white flower is striking and hard to spot because it only grows at high altitude (1800–3300m).

Houseleek: A beautiful pink flower which grows on rocks above 1600m. It blooms in August.

Alpine Poppy: This bright yellow flower loves limestone scree and blooms in July/August.

Alpenrose

Edelweiss

Houseleek

Alpine Willowherb

Gentian

Alpine Poppy

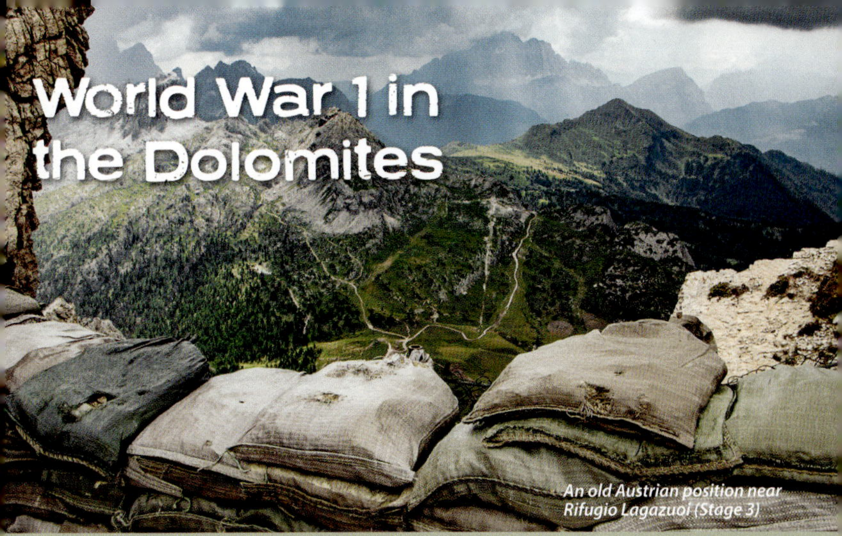

An old Austrian position near Rifugio Lagazuoi (Stage 3)

The Dolomites saw much fighting and bloodshed during WW1 (1914-1918). In May 1915, Italy entered the 'Great War' on the side of the Allies (Britain, France and Russia) by declaring war on the Austro-Hungarian (or Habsburg) Empire. Italy was the only one of the main Allies which did not claim to be fighting for defensive reasons: rather it was an aggressor, hoping to seize territory (including the Dolomites) from Austria. The Allies were desperate to bring Italy into the war so they agreed to award territory to it in the event of victory. As a consequence, Winston Churchill described Italy as the 'harlot of Europe'.

The fighting was conducted along the 600km Italy-Austria border which then passed through the Dolomites. The Italians arrogantly expected to be in Vienna by Christmas but in fact, notwithstanding 651,000 dead, they only took about 30km of ground over the next three years.

The Italian army was originally led by Luigi Cadorna, a stubborn and arrogant man, who had an unshakeable belief in the tactics of the 'frontal assault', irrespective of the fire-power of his opponents. As a result, the Italians stuck firmly to a strategy of huge infantry charges, oblivious to the tactical implications of the Austrian barbed-wire, machine guns and trench network. The mountainous terrain ruthlessly exploited the flaws in this strategy: the Austrian front-line was often sensibly positioned at height allowing Austrian troops to inflict huge damage upon the Italians who attacked in long lines from below.

This was particularly true in the Dolomites where the Austrians fell back tactically from the true border to cliffs, ridges and peaks far above the access roads. After the Austrians abandoned Cortina d'Ampezzo without a fight, the Italians advanced W and in June 1915 reached Passo Falzàrego (which is just below Rifugio Lagazuoi (Stage 3)). The Austrians were well dug into the cliffs above the pass and many of their emplacements can still be seen on Stage 3. Pinned to the cliffs below to shelter from the Austrian fire, the Italians were unable to advance further N to the nearby Passo di Valparola. Soon they were living in huts fixed to ledges in the cliffs above the valley floor. They were supplied by cables and incredibly, they scaled the cracks and fissures in the rocks to attack the Austrians. Sometimes they bolted ladders into the rock-face, many of which are still used today on the region's many via ferrata routes (see page 47).

Having made little progress, the Italians decided to dig tunnels through the mountains up to the Austrian positions so that they could lay mines. Many of these tunnels can still be

WW1 trenches right beside the AV1 on Stage 4a

visited today, including the Lagazuoi tunnel which can actually be used to travel to Passo Falzàrego as an AV1 alternative route (see Stage 4a).

Still unable to break through to Passo di Valparola, the Italians decided to try to head through the Travenànzes Valley via Forcella Col dei Bòs, a mountain pass which is crossed on Stage 4a. Unfortunately, the pass was overlooked by the Austrian positions on il Castelletto which is a rock outcrop beside the mountain of Tofana de Rozes. Il Castelletto held a whole platoon in its tunnels and caves and could be resupplied in safety at night. In late 1915, the Italians hatched a plan to mine il Castelletto: they would dig a 500m tunnel to it from the foot of Tofana de Rozes (which they had captured in the autumn). The mine itself would consist of 35 tonnes of gelignite. 120 soldiers (who had worked as miners before the war) toiled around the clock in shifts clearing up to 6m each day. The Italians also dug a subsidiary tunnel inside Tofana de Rozes from which the soldiers would access il Castelletto after the mine was detonated. Meanwhile the Austrians had started to dig a counter-mine.

The King of Italy was watching from across the valley as the Italian mine was detonated: it blew the top off the southern part of the summit of Tofana de Rozes. The Italian soldiers either succumbed to carbon monoxide from the blast, were crushed by rocks or were repelled by Austrian fire. The next day though, the Italians captured the S side of il Castelletto but they still failed to advance down the Travenànzes Valley. The Austrians had cleverly retreated and prepared a new defensive line: they ambushed the Italians who incurred heavy losses. It took three more months to capture the N side of il Castelletto.

Conditions endured by soldiers in the Dolomites were severe and it was the first time that war had been fought at such high altitudes. The mountains were covered with snow for significant periods of the year and temperatures dropped as low as -40°C. Frostbite and snow-blindness were common. Many positions were so isolated that during the winter the only means of supply was by cable-ways from the valleys below. On Marmolada where snow remained all year round, barracks were actually dug into the ice. And then there were the avalanches which killed more soldiers than bullets or shells: on 13 December 1916 alone, 10,000 soldiers died in avalanches.

WW1 memorial near Forcella Col dei Bòs

The Italian soldiers were not well-treated by their own army: they were badly paid, badly fed, badly trained and badly equipped. Ultimately, they shed blood, sweat and tears in vain: the Austrians defences were so well-positioned that the Italians could make little headway. Despite using all the technology and engineering genius available to them, the Italians were effectively defeated by the mountains themselves.

Although Italy succeeded in gaining substantial territory when the Habsburg empire was broken-up (see 'Italian or German?' below), the war had a disastrous long-term impact. Italy's liberal parties were completely discredited by the war and the subsequent negotiations, and were soon overthrown by the fascist regime of Benito Mussolini.

Italian or German?

Descending towards Rifugio Pian de Fontana (Stage 10)

The AV1 passes through two regions of Italy: the Trentino in the S and Alto Adige in the N. In 1815 both of these areas came under Austrian control, causing much resentment in Italy. In 1915, Italy agreed to enter WW1 on the side of the Allies. In return, the Allies promised Italy possession of certain lands (including the Trentino and Alto Adige) after the war was won. Accordingly, in 1919 these two regions were transferred to Italy where they remain to this day.

As was so often the case in the colonial era, the ethnic origins of the populations were overlooked when drawing international frontiers. A census in 1910 had declared that while only 3.5% of the population of the Trentino was German-speaking, only 6.8% of the population of Alto Adige was Italian-speaking. The 1919 transfer to Italy made an estimated 250,000 German-speakers subject to Italian rule. Afterwards, under Mussolini's fascist regime, a policy of repression was implemented against the German-speakers of Alto Adige, including the confiscation of property and the abolition of personal rights and freedom of speech. Place names were systematically 'Italianised' and Italian war veterans were sent to live there. Eventually, however, these measures were relaxed to avoid offending the Nazi government in Germany.

Along the AV1, the cultural differences are still tangible today. Each town, village and rifugio has both an Italian and a German name which is often confusing for the visitor. Both German and Italian are widely spoken. And restaurants often serve both Austrian and Italian food.

Via Ferrata

The via ferrata on Stage v11

The optional Stage v11 is a 'via ferrata' route. Via ferrata is an Italian phrase which literally means 'iron road'. The term dates back to WW1, when steel ladders were bolted into rock-faces in the Dolomites to assist with the movement of troops. In recent decades, these old routes have been repaired and are still used by hikers and climbers. Modern routes have also been constructed.

A via ferrata enables people with no rock-climbing experience to ascend a rock-face with the assistance of ladders, steps and cables (onto which the user should be clipped at all times). If attempting Stage v11, you should be properly equipped with a climbing harness, twin lanyard and carabiner set, helmet and gloves. Furthermore, you should know how to use this equipment: get instruction beforehand from an experienced professional unless you know what you are doing.

Tackling Stage v11 is an exhilarating experience which is a highlight of the AV1, but it should not be treated lightly and should not be attempted by anyone who does not have a good head for heights. A fall during a via ferrata can lead to serious injury or even death. Full detail on how to undertake a via ferrata is beyond the scope of this book.

Route Summary

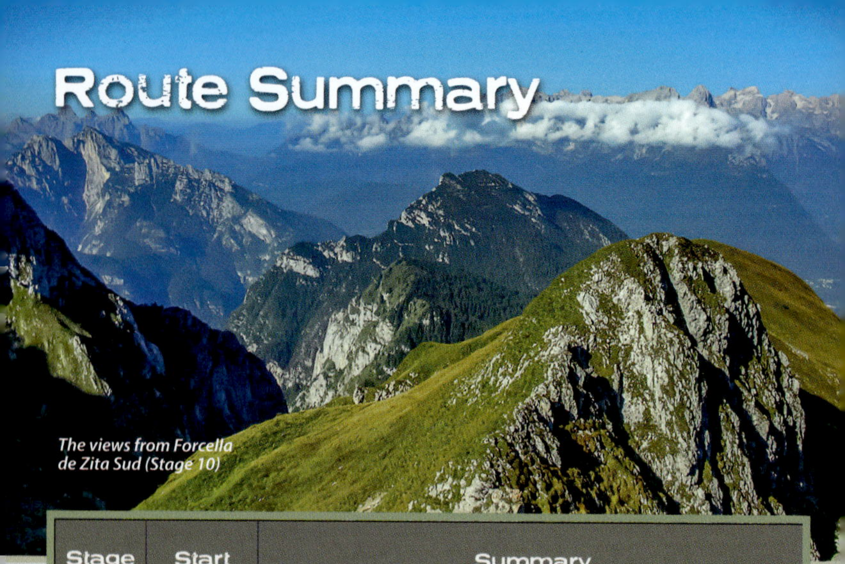

The views from Forcella de Zita Sud (Stage 10)

Stage	Start	Summary
1	Lago di Braies	An incredible introduction to the AV1 with perhaps the finest opening 20min of any Alpine trek: it starts with a heavenly walk around the exquisite Lago di Braies. Afterwards, there is a long climb through starkly beautiful terrain. The top of the climb is only a stone's throw from the historic Rifugio Biella.
2a	Rifugio Biella	Start with a gentle descent (on an old military 'road') through the barren moonscape around Rifugio Biella. Soon, however, leave the broad track for a path winding through a spectacular zone of grassy hillocks. Finish the stage with a short descent to the modern Rifugio Sennes.
2b	Rifugio Sennes	The first sustained descent of the AV1 takes place on broad tracks. Enjoy the wonderful scenery as you head across pastures and down through forest: the pale limestone rock of the nearby peaks is always in sight. The stage terminates at the busy Rifugio Pederü.
2c	Rifugio Pederü	Probably, the most stunning section of the AV1 so far. After a steep start, the path levels and winds through classic Dolomite terrain offering incredible views of the nearby jagged peaks. The pale limestone rock contrasts sharply with the beautiful green vegetation and the deep blue sky. A second, more gentle, climb leads to Rifugio Fanes.
3	Rifugio Fanes	A highlight of the AV1. A short climb brings you to a magnificent hanging valley: for a few sublime km you stroll amongst green pastures and jagged peaks with interesting geology. Afterwards, however, the stage becomes more difficult: there is a long climb to a high pass. Over the pass, the terrain changes dramatically: soft, grassy slopes give way to stark, barren rock. After a challenging descent, start the long climb to Rifugio Lagazuoi, the highest point on the AV1.

Stage	Start	Summary
4a	Rifugio Lagazuoi	Enter stark but spectacular terrain which is typical of the northern Dolomites: pale, jagged peaks enclose valleys and plateaus of limestone and grass. As you descend, the terrain gets softer with less rock and more grass. Ever-present are a selection of stunning Dolomite walls and summits. There is plenty of history here too as you will pass the scenes of famous WW1 battles.
4b	Rifugio Dibona	Descend through forest and then climb to the famous Cinque Torri ('five towers'), a stunning rock formation. Rifugio Cinque Torri is situated just below the towers. It serves some of the best food on the AV1.
4c	Rifugio Cinque Torri	A short climb to two of the most famous rifugi on the AV1: Rifugio Averau with its legendary cooking and Rifugio Nuvolau with its legendary sunset views. The route also passes close to Rifugio Scoiattoli which has a wonderful setting looking over the Cinque Torri.
5a	Rifugio Nuvolau	This is one of the most talked about sections of the AV1. From the rifugio, head across rock: the views are exquisite in all directions. Soon, arrive at the crux of the stage: the two exposed descents with cables bolted into the rock to assist. As you descend, the rock gives way to grass and you enter some of the finest scenery on the AV1.
5b	Rifugio Passo Giau	An incredible traverse takes you across grassy slopes decked with wildflowers and surrounded by magnificent peaks. Many passes are crossed on this stage, each of which offers stunning views. After Forcella Giau, enter a Dolomite wonderland of green pastures and limestone where the unusual angles of the mountains are unforgettable. After Forcella Ambrizzola, traverse a barren zone of white limestone and then start the long descent to the popular Rifugio Città di Fiume.
v5	Croda da Lago Variant	This variant is not as scenic as the main AV1 but it is still lovely. Rifugio Croda da Lago has a magnificent setting beside Lago de Federa and is a fabulous place to stay: because it is tucked away on an AV1 variant, it is often very peaceful, attracting fewer overnight visitors.
6a	Rifugio Città di Fiume	A short but spectacular stage which traverses the NW slopes of the famous Pelmo (3168m). You pass right next to the mountain: the sheer cliffs are breathtaking. Afterwards, descend through forest to Rifugio Passo Staulanza.
6b	Rifugio Passo Staulanza	This link route travels between the Pelmo and the Civetta. As you proceed, the views back towards the Pelmo get better and better, culminating with the incredible viewpoint at Rifugio Coldai. The sunset at the rifugio is divine.

Stage	Start	Summary
v6	Rifugio Venezia Variant	An exceptional (but challenging) variant making a clockwise circumnavigation of the Pelmo: the views are breathtaking, particularly at Forcella Val d'Arcia. Rifugio Venezia, about half-way along the stage, is a spectacular place to stay and the sunsets are magnificent.
7a	Rifugio Coldai	This stage is another highlight of the AV1. A short climb brings you to Forcella Coldai where you catch sight of the scenic Lago Coldai. Next an amazing balcony path skirts below the cliffs of the Civetta: a humbling experience. Finally, climb to Rifugio Tissi which has sublime views of the Civetta.
7b	Rifugio Tissi	The descent to Rifugio Vazzoler takes you through a glorious world of pastures and pine trees as you head around the strikingly pale peaks of the Civetta's southern extremity. Rifugio Vazzoler is a great place for an overnight break.
8a	Rifugio Vazzoler	A sublime journey amongst jagged limestone peaks which are bright white against the backdrop of the deep blue sky. Most of the stage is spent on astonishing balcony paths as you skirt the S flanks of the Moiazza group of mountains.
8b	Rifugio Bruto Carestiato	A short stage, descending E to the road-head at Passo Duran. Enjoy far-reaching views to the S. To the E, the peak of Cima Nord di San Sebastiano dominates.
9	Passo Duran	After a climb through forest, cross an enormous ravine on a narrow path: the scenery is wonderful with the colours of the pale limestone rock, beautiful vegetation and deep blue skies complimenting each other perfectly. Keep climbing and cross a magnificent pass which offers some of the finest views on the whole trek. An undulating path then makes its way down to a fabulous rifugio with a fabulous setting.
10	Rifugio Pramperet	This is the wildest stage of the main AV1 with some of the finest mountain scenery in Europe. For many, it will be the highlight of the whole trek. However, these delights are hard-earned: the climb starts straight out of the blocks and is very steep. The crux of the stage is an exhilarating climb up a knife-edge ridge, leading to a magnificent mountain pass. Afterwards, the first part of the descent to the rifugio is an exceptionally scenic wander through an exquisite grassy valley filled with wild-flowers. The second part of the descent is very steep and requires concentration.
11a	Rifugio Pian de Fontana	The AV1 is drawing to a close and this stage provides the last great views. A short descent and then a short climb bring you to Forcella la Varéta. Afterwards, a heavenly traverse around the grassy slopes offers wonderful views into Val Vescovà where you will find the comfortable Rifugio Bianchet.

Stage	Start	Summary
11b	Rifugio Bianchet	A beautiful and easy descent to conclude the AV1. Although you head through forest, there are still some lovely mountain views. The path brings you to the road near la Pissa where you can catch a bus to Belluno
v11	Via Ferrata Variant	This variant is by far the most difficult part of the AV1 but it makes for an awesome climax to the trek. A long, tough climb through wild and remote terrain brings you to the sublime Forcella del Marmol. Here the real fun begins because this is the start of a two hour via ferrata: an exposed route through beautiful mountain terrain, assisted by metal ladders and cables bolted into the rock-face.

The climb to Forcella del Moschesin (Stage 9)

Cima di Pramper (Stage 10)

Route Description

1
Pragser Wildsee
Lago di Bràies
Pragser Wildsee
Lago di Braies
GR. APOSTEL
KL. APOSTEL
Grünwaldalm
Malga Foresta
DI FORESTA
SEEWALD
Seeweg
Stage 1
KL. SEEKOFEL
SEEKOFEL
SAS DLA PORTA
CRODA DEL BECO
OFEN
FORNO
OFENMAUER
M. MURO
CIANPO ROS
Forc. Sora Forno
Ofenscharte
Rif. Biella
alla Croda del Beco
Seekofelhütte
CRODA DE
Stage 2a
Continued on Map 2a
©Tabacco SRL 2019
0
1km

Lago di Braies/ Pragser Wildsee to Rifugio Biella

1

The magnificent view from Forcella Sora Forno

An incredible introduction to the AV1 with perhaps the finest opening 20min of any Alpine trek: it starts with a heavenly walk around the exquisite Lago di Braies. Afterwards, things get a bit more serious as there is a long, steep climb through starkly beautiful terrain: a shock to the system so early in the trek. Fortunately, however, the stage is not too long and the top of the climb is only a stone's throw from the historic Rifugio Biella. This mountain hut may be spartan but it is atmospheric: nowadays there are not many of these 'old school' huts left.

The route mostly uses good paths, however, there are some sections of shale. There is also one short, steep section over rocks which has a cable to assist: this is slippery if wet. Navigation is straightforward as the stage is well marked.

Time	3:15
Distance	6.9
Ascent	929
Descent	96
Max Altitude	2389
Refreshments	Rifugio Biella
Accommodation	Rifugio Biella
Path Numbers	1

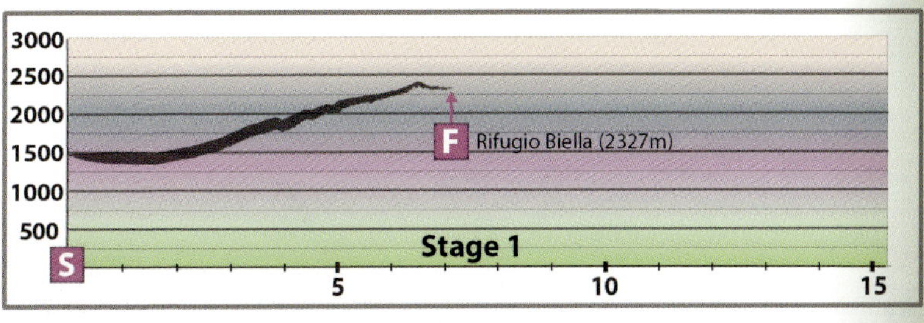

The remarkable Lago di Braies

The path leading to Rifugio Biella

S See Map 1. Pass to the left of **Hotel Lago di Braies** onto a beach: technically the beach is not on the AV1 (which officially runs behind the hotel) but it offers probably the best view of the lake. TR and walk S along the beach to a lovely chapel. Then follow Path 1 along the W side of the lake.

1 0:15: TL just before a wooden toilet and head around the S shore of the lake. 5-10min later, TR and climb on a shale path away from the lake.

2 1:40: After descending briefly, TR at a junction. 10min later, ignore a faint path on the left.

3 2:25: Climb steeply across rocks (which can be slippery): there are cables to assist. 5min later, enter a barren plateau. TR at a junction.

4 3:05: Keep SH across **Forcella Sora Forno (2389m)**: the path on the right leads to the summit of Croda del Beco (2810m).

F 3:15: Arrive at **Rifugio Biella/Seekofelhütte (2327m)**.

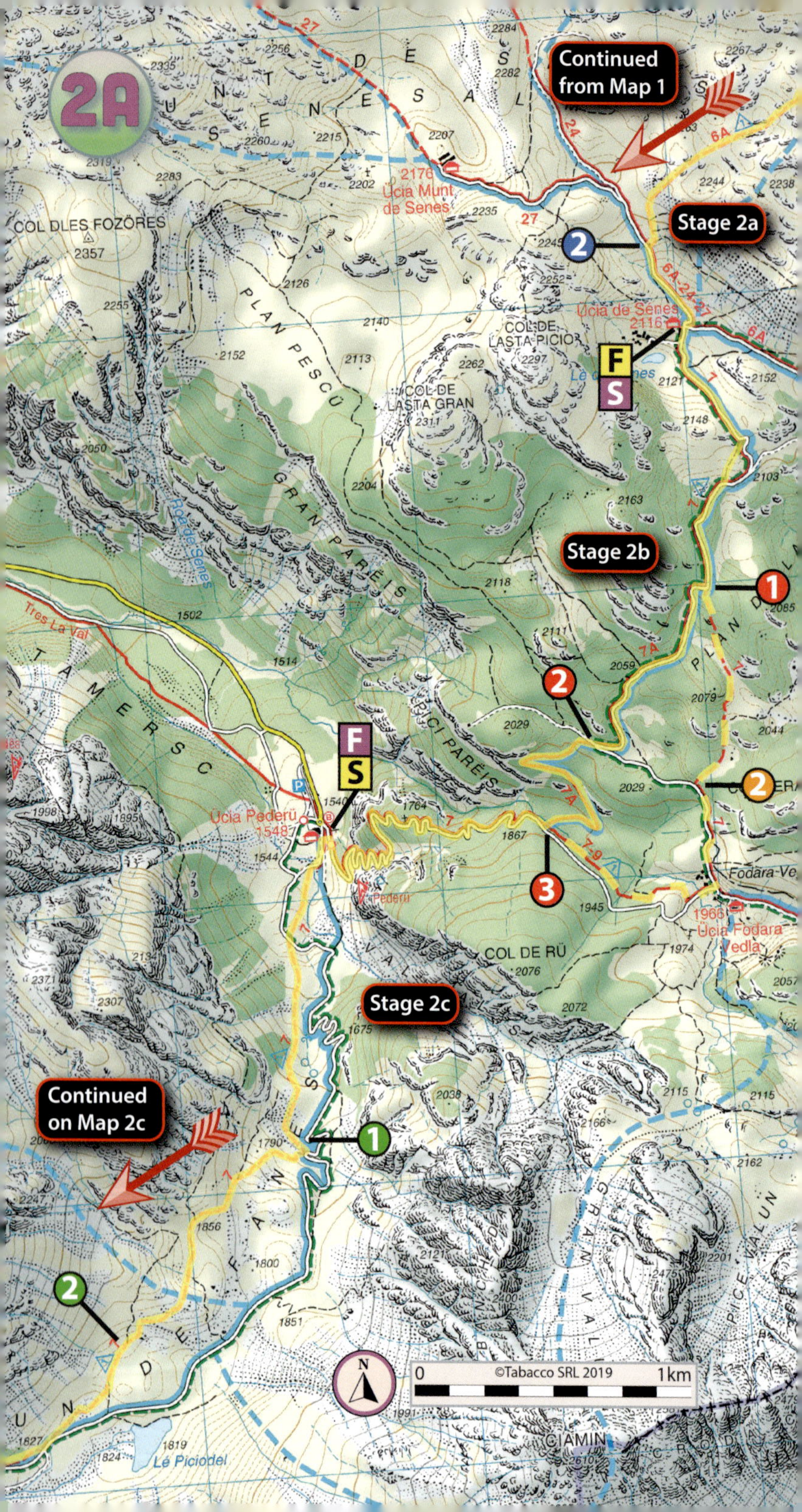

2A
Continued from Map 1
Stage 2a
Stage 2b
Stage 2c
Continued on Map 2c
Ücia Munt de Senes
Ücia de Senes
Ücia Pederü
Ücia Fodara Vedla
COL DLES FOZÖRES
PLAN PESCÜ
GRAN PAREIS
PICI PAREIS
COL DE LASTA PICIO
COL DE LASTA GRAN
COL DE RÜ
Tres La Val
Fodara-Ve
Lé Piciodel
CIAMIN
©Tabacco SRL 2019
1km

Rifugio Biella to Rifugio Sennes

2A

Rifugio Sennes is more modern than Rifugio Biella

Start with a gentle descent (on an old military 'road') through the barren moonscape around Rifugio Biella. Soon, however, leave the broad track for a path winding through a spectacular zone of grassy hillocks. Finish the stage with a short descent to the modern Rifugio Sennes.

Navigation and terrain are generally straightforward except that the surface of the path on the descent to the rifugio is sometimes steep and rocky.

Time	1:00
Distance	3.1
Ascent	53
Descent	264
Max Altitude	2327
Refreshments	Rifugio Sennes
Accommodation	Rifugio Sennes
Path Numbers	6 → 6A

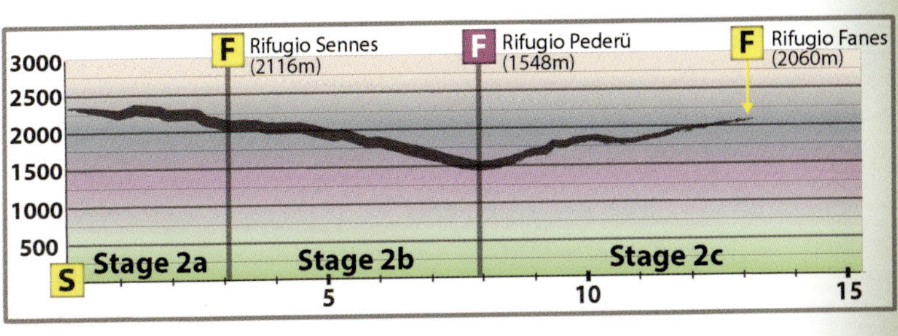

Cross a beautiful zone of grassy hillocks soon after leaving Rifugio Biella

S See Map 1. Head W on a broad track (Path 6) which is an old military 'road'.

1 0:20: TR at a junction onto Path 6A (the more southerly of two paths on the right). Climb briefly and soon head through grassy hillocks.

2 0:55: See Map 2A. After a short rocky descent, TL at a junction onto a track.

F 1:00: 5min later, arrive at **Rifugio Sennes/Ücia de Senes (2116m)**.

Rifugio Sennes to Rifugio Pederü

2B

Rifugio Pederü

Fortunately, the first sustained descent of the AV1 takes place on broad tracks. For the most part, you can relax and enjoy the wonderful scenery as you head across pastures and down through forest: the pale limestone rock of the nearby peaks is always in sight. The stage terminates at the busy Rifugio Pederü. Navigation is straightforward. Parts of the descent are very steep.

As an alternative to Rifugio Pederü, you could stay at the more peaceful Rifugio Fodara Vedla: this detour adds only 10-15min to the stage (see below).

If you wish to join or leave the AV1 at Rifugio Pederü, bus 462 runs to St. Vigil/S. Vigilio (see www.sad.it for timetables). From St. Vigil, buses head to St. Lorenzen/S. Lorenzo where there are rail connections.

Time	1:45
Distance	4.8
Ascent	0
Descent	568
Max Altitude	2116
Refreshments	Rifugio Fodara Vedla Rifugio Pederü
Accommodation	Rifugio Fodara Vedla Rifugio Pederü
Path Numbers	7 → 7A → 7

2B

Much of the stage uses WW1 military 'roads'

S See Map 2A. Head S on a track (Path 7): alternatively, use a popular grassy path, to the left of the track, which is more direct. 5min later, TR onto a path and descend. A few minutes later, TR onto the track again.

1 0:30: At a junction, remain on the track (now Path 7A), ignoring a path to the left: alternatively, take this path (Path 7) if you wish to use the Rifugio Fodara Vedla Detour (see below).

2 0:50: TR and leave the track: just afterwards, take the most southerly of two paths (the one on the left).

3 1:05: Keep SH at a junction: this is where the Rifugio Fodara Vedla Detour rejoins the main AV1.

F 1:45: Arrive at **Rifugio Pederü (1548m)**.

Rifugio Fodara Vedla Detour

1 At Waypoint No.1, TL to leave the track and descend on Path 7.

2 0:50: TL onto a track. 10min later, arrive at **Rifugio Fodara Vedla (1966m)**. Head W on Path 7.

3 1:15: Keep SH, rejoining the main AV1.

F 1:55: Arrive at **Rifugio Pederü (1548m)**.

Rifugio Pederü to Rifugio Fanes

2C

Ütia Pices Fanes

Probably, the most beautiful section of the AV1 so far. After a steep start, the path levels and winds through classic Dolomite terrain offering incredible views of the nearby jagged peaks. The pale limestone rock contrasts sharply with the beautiful green vegetation and the deep blue sky. A second, more gentle, climb leads to Rifugio Fanes which has an excellent 'à la carte' restaurant.

There are few waymarks on this stage and occasionally, there are unmarked junctions: keep to the main path, ignoring offshoots. As an alternative to Rifugio Fanes, you could stay at the superb Rifugio Lavarella: this detour adds only 15-20min to the AV1 (see below).

Time	2:00
Distance	5.2
Ascent	560
Descent	48
Max Altitude	2060
Refreshments	Ütia Pices Fanes Rifugio Fanes Rifugio Lavarella
Accommodation	Ücia dles Muntagnoles Rifugio Fanes Rifugio Lavarella
Path Numbers	7 → 11

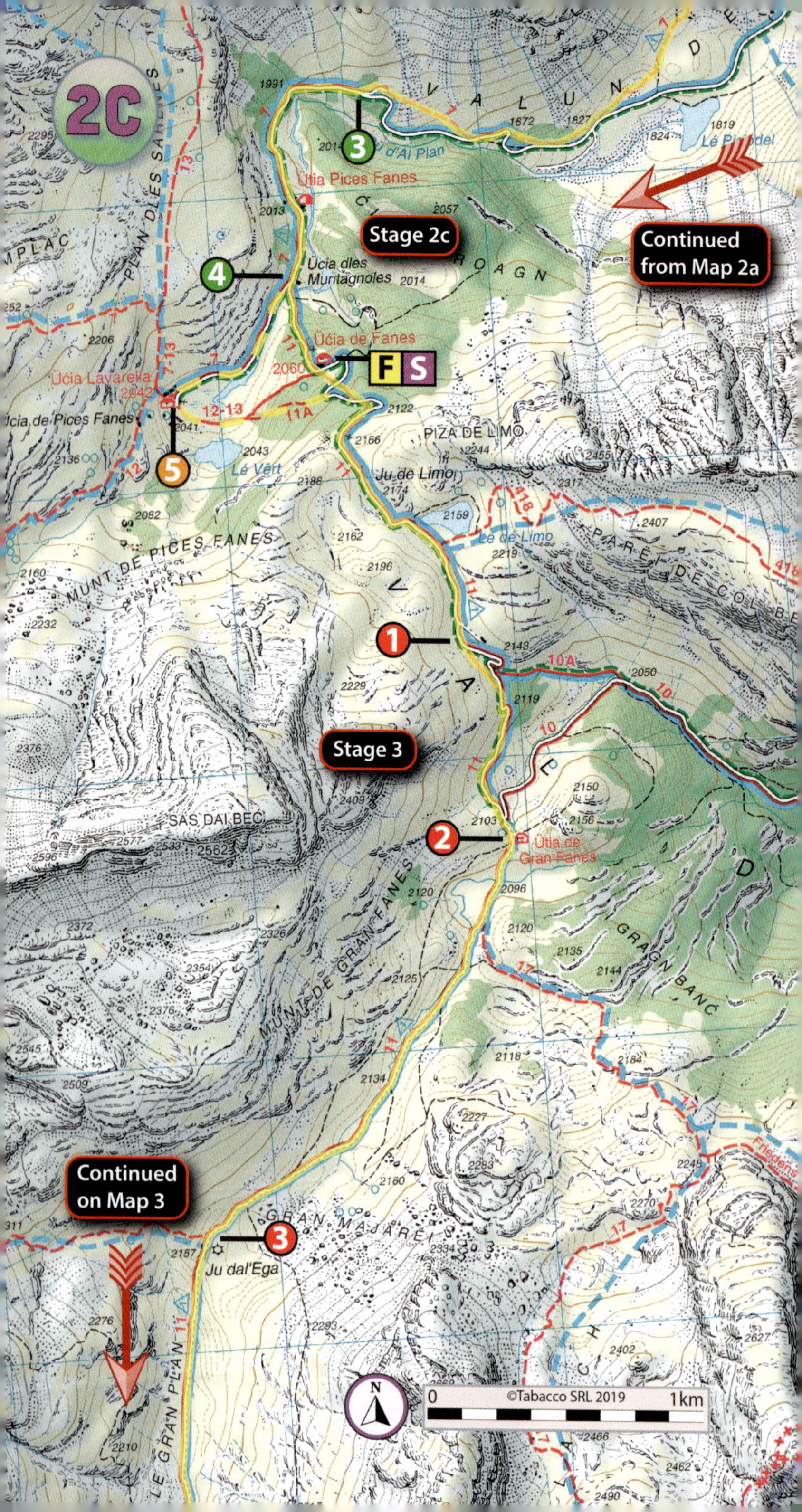
2C
Stage 2c
Continued from Map 2a
Stage 3
Continued on Map 3
Ütia Pices Fanes
Ücia dles Muntagnoles
Ücia de Fanes
Ücia Lavarela
Ücia de Pices Fanes
Ütia de Gran Fanes
Lé Vërt
Lé de Limo
Lé Piciodel
PIZA DE LIMO
Ju de Limo
MUNT DE PICES FANES
MUNT DE GRAN FANES
SAS DAI BEC
GRAN MAJAREI
Ju dal'Ega
PLAN DLES SAROES
LE GRAN PLAN
GRAGN BANC
PARE DE COL BE
VAL UN DE
F
S
©Tabacco SRL 2019
0
1km

2C

Enjoy classic Dolomite scenery on the way to Rifugio Fanes

S See Map 2A. Head S on Path 7. Shortly afterwards, cross a bridge. Immediately afterwards, TL on a path. A few minutes later, keep SH across a track.

1 0:35: When the path meets a track, turn sharp right onto another path and climb steeply: keep on the main path, ignoring offshoots.

2 1:10: Keep SH across a plateau: the path is faint. Shortly afterwards, when you arrive at a track, TR onto a path ('Fanes') and climb.

3 1:40: See Map 2C. Keep SH on a track. 10min later, pass a little restaurant, **Ütia Pices Fanes**.

4 1:55: 5min later, arrive at **Ücia dles Muntagnoles**, a little rifugio with 4 rooms which offers bed and breakfast. Beside the rifugio, there is a junction: TL to head to Rifugio Fanes (Path 11). Alternatively, TR on Path 7 for the Rifugio Lavarella Detour (see below).

F 2:00: Arrive at **Rifugio Fanes (2060m)**.

Rifugio Lavarella Detour

4 1:55: At Waypoint No.4, TR on Path 7.

5 2:05: Arrive at **Rifugio Lavarella (2042m)**.

To return to the main AV1, head E from Rifugio Lavarella on Path 12-13. After 5min, TR at a fork onto Path 11A. 5-10min later, TR at a track to rejoin the AV1.

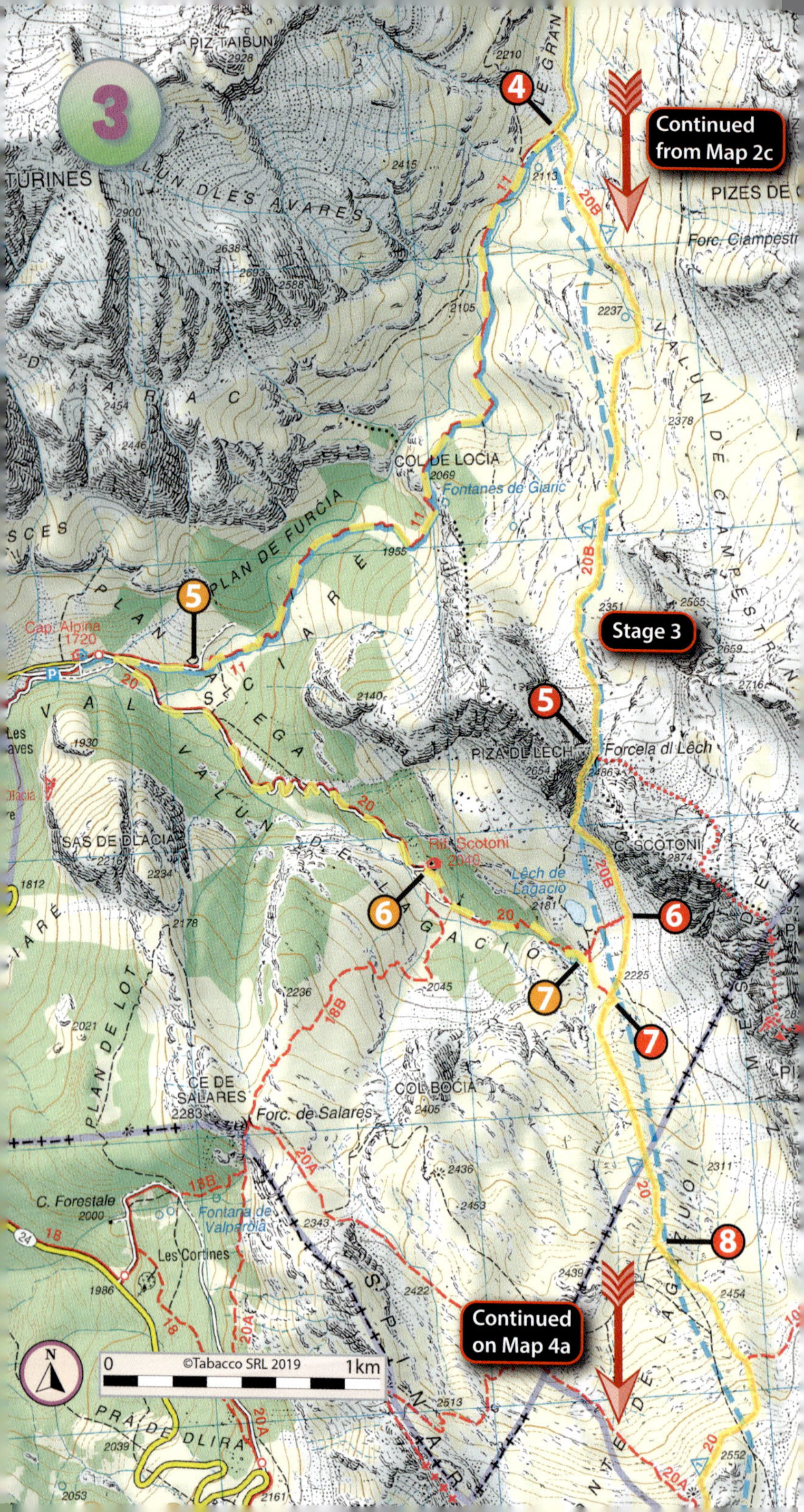
3
Continued from Map 2c
Stage 3
Continued on Map 4a
©Tabacco SRL 2019
0
1km
PIZ TAIBUN
TURINES
LUN DLES AVARES
PIZES DE
Forc. Ciampestr
VALUN DE CIAMPESTRIN
COL DE LOCIA
Fontanes de Giaric
PLAN DE FURCIA
Cap. Alpina 1720
PLAN
ALCEGA
VAL
VALUN DE LAGACIO
Forcela dl Lêch
PIZA DE LECH
C. SCOTONI
Rif. Scotoni 2040
Lêch de Lagacio
SAS DE DLACIA
PLAN DE LOT
CE DE SALARES
Forc. de Salares
COL BOCIA
C. Forestale 2000
Fontana de Valparola
Les Cortines
PRA DE DLIRA

Rifugio Fanes to Rifugio Lagazuoi

3

The statue of an eagle at Rifugio Fanes

On a fine day, this stage is a highlight of the AV1. A short climb brings you to a magnificent hanging valley where Ütia de Gran Fanes (a small refugio) is superbly located. Relax as you follow an easy path through the valley: for a few sublime km you stroll amongst green pastures and jagged peaks with interesting geology. Afterwards, however, the stage becomes more difficult: there is a long climb to a high pass, Forcela dl Lêch. The scenery is incredible.

Across the pass, the terrain changes dramatically: soft, grassy slopes give way to stark, barren rock. At first glance, the descent from the pass, through a precipitous gully, seems barely possible. However, look more closely and you will see the path zigzagging downwards. At the bottom, start the long climb to Rifugio Lagazuoi, the highest point on the AV1.

This is a challenging stage with a lot of climbing. The last few metres of the climb to Forcela dl Lêch are steep and tricky: you must cross a short section of rocks. Furthermore, the descent from the pass is one of the hardest sections of the AV1: take great care as a fall could be serious. You can avoid Forcela dl Lêch by taking the Rifugio Scotoni Detour (see below) which takes about 3hr to rejoin the AV1 near Lêch de Lagaciò. In fact, this detour is very beautiful in its own right and Rifugio Scotoni is a wonderful place to stay: a useful alternative if Rifugio Lagazuoi is full.

There is a cable car station beside Rifugio Lagazuoi: if you wish to leave the AV1, you could use it to descend to the road at Passo Falzàrego. From there, catch bus 30/31 to Cortina d'Ampezzo (to the E) or la Villa/ Stern (to the W): for timetables see www.dolomitibus.it.

The magnificent hanging valley after Ütia de Gran Fanes

Time	5:30
Distance	12.7
Ascent	1069
Descent	377
Max Altitude	2752
Refreshments	Ütia de Gran Fanes. Rifugio Scotoni Rifugio Lagazuoi
Accommodation	Ütia de Gran Fanes. Rifugio Scotoni Rifugio Lagazuoi
Path Numbers	11 → 20B → 20 → 401

3

The stage starts with an easy walk on more WWI military roads

3

One of the WW1 bunkers near Rifugio Lagazuoi

S See Map 2C. Climb SE on Path 11, heading into trees. 5min later, TL onto a track.

1 0:25: TR onto a path. A few minutes later, TR onto the track again. 10min later, keep SH at a junction.

2 0:45: Just afterwards, arrive at **Ütia de Gran Fanes**. Head SW on Path 11. A few minutes later, TR at a fork and head through an incredible hanging valley, climbing gently.

3 1:30: TL at a fork.

4 1:45: See Map 3. TL at a junction (Path 20B) and climb.

5 2:45: Just before the top, there is a short section of rocks to negotiate. Cross **Forcela dl Lêch (2486m)** and descend steeply, zigzagging down a rocky gully: take great care.

6 3:30: At a faint junction just above a lake (Lêch de Lagaciò), keep SH: do not TR and descend towards the lake. 5min later, TR at a faint junction (easy to miss): look out for a WW1 ruin just to the right.

7 3:35: Just afterwards, TL onto Path 20 and start the long climb to the rifugio which you should see far above.

8 4:20: Keep SH at a faint junction. 10min later, TL at a fork: confusingly, the signpost claims that you are on Path 401 but the waymarks indicate that it is still Path 20. Shortly afterwards, notice the WW1 bunkers carved into the mountains. At any junctions, keep following 'No.20' signs and waymarks.

9 5:00: See Map 4A. TR at **Forcela Lagazuói (2573m)** onto Path 401. Climb steeply, soon passing WW1 bunkers: most have fallen into disrepair but there are a few near the rifugio which have been restored.

F 5:30: Arrive at **Rifugio Lagazuoi (2752m)**.

Rifugio Scotoni Detour

4 1:45: See Map 3. At Waypoint No.4, keep SH on Path 11. After **Col de Locia (2069m)** descend generally SW.

5 3:05: Keep SH on a track. 5min later, TL onto Path 20, climbing SE: alternatively, keep SH for **Camping Saas Dlacia** (1.3km).

6 4:10: Keep SH past **Rifugio Scotoni (2040m)** still climbing SE on Path 20.

7 4:40: TR at a junction. 5min later, rejoin the main AV1 at red Waypoint No.7: continue climbing on Path 20.

Rifugio Lagazuoi to Rifugio Dibona

4A

Walkers at Forcella Col dei Bòs

Shortly after leaving the rifugio, enter starkly beautiful terrain which is typical of the northern Dolomites: pale, jagged peaks enclose valleys and plateaus of limestone and grass. As you descend, the terrain gets softer with less rock and more grass. Ever-present are a selection of stunning Dolomite walls and summits.

There is plenty of history here too as you will pass the scenes of the battle for il Castelletto, one of the most famous events of WW1 that took place in the Dolomites (see page 45). The route passes the head of the Travenànzes Valley, crosses Forcella Col dei Bòs and traverses below il Castelletto itself and the nearby summit of Tofana de Rozes: these places are where the action played out. Trenches, ruined barracks and rusted debris from the war are all still visible today, right beside the path. The famous tunnel dug by the Italians to mine il Castelletto is also quite close to the path as you traverse the slopes of Tofana de Rozes: you can climb up and view the entrance to the tunnel but to enter it you will need via ferrata equipment and the appropriate experience.

The terrain on the Tofana de Rozes traverse is rocky and sometimes unstable: take care on a particularly delicate section which crosses a gully. The drops here are steep. After this traverse, the descent to Rifugio Dibona is steep and rocky in places.

Navigation on the stage is sometimes tricky, particularly around the nebulous Forcella Col dei Bòs: the signposts there are confusing and there is a labyrinth of different paths. Markings are sparse and often hard to spot. Follow the directions closely.

The peaks on the W flank of the Travenànzes Valley

Stages 4a and 4b can be avoided using one of the following alternatives:

1. **Direct route to Rifugio Averau using the cable car:** Descend from Rifugio Lagazuoi to Passo Falzàrego (2105m) using the cable car. Cross the road and pick up Path 441, heading SE. Soon climb, sometimes on a path and sometimes on a track. 1hr20min from Passo Falzàrego, keep SH across Forcella Averau (2435m). 20min later, arrive back on the AV1 at Rifugio Averau (2413m).

2. **Direct route to Rifugio Averau using the WW1 tunnels:** Galleria Lagazuoi was dug by the Italians to attack Austrian positions during WW1. It runs inside the mountain for more than 1 km and has been completely restored. Although it is classed as a beginners' via ferrata and is equipped with cables, it is technically undemanding. Most people do it without via ferrata equipment although a helmet is useful to protect your head from the low rock ceilings. It is unsuitable for those with claustrophobia. The darkness is only interrupted by a few windows cut into the rock so you will need a flashlight.

   To locate the tunnel, head back downhill from Rifugio Lagazuoi. TR just after the cable car station. 10min later, enter the tunnel using a wooden doorway. Descend steeply using steps, ladders and cables. After about 1hr, emerge at a ledge. After a gully and another shorter tunnel, TR onto Path 402: follow it down to Passo Falzàrego (1hr30min from Rifugio Lagazuoi). From there, follow Alternative No.1 above to Rifugio Averau.

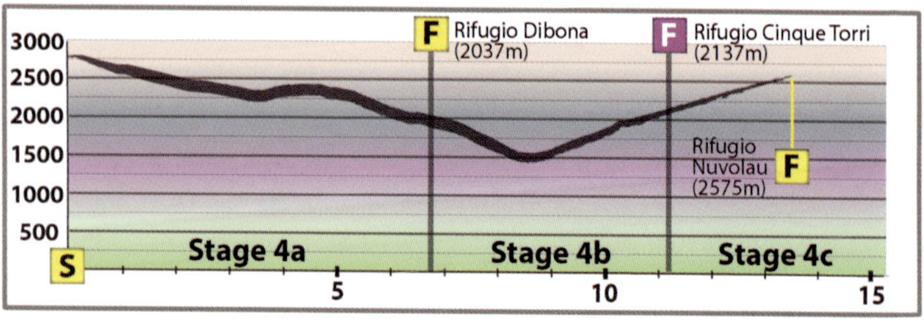

The Travenànzes Valley

S See Map 4A. Retrace your steps back down to **Forcela Lagazuói (2573m)**: TR on Path 401. Keep SH on the main path, ignoring offshoots.

1 0:35: TL at **Forcella Travenànzes (2507m)**, still on Path 401: do not go hard left onto Path 20. As you continue, the Travenànzes Valley is on the left. Tofana de Rozes and il Castelletto are straight ahead.

2 0:55: Just after crossing a stream bed, TR at a junction onto Path 402, heading E. Shortly afterwards, TL at a faint junction, following waymarks: navigation is tricky in this area and the signposts are confusing.

3 1:10: At a junction at **Forcella Col dei Bòs (2332m)**, TR onto Path 402: beside the path, there is a WW1 memorial and debris left over from the war. Just afterwards, notice the WW1 trenches. A few minutes later, TL onto Path 404 which traverses underneath Tofana de Rozes: soon, if you wish to view the tunnel (Galleria del Castelletto), take one of the paths heading up to the left.

After a while, cross a huge gully: take care as the path is narrow and unstable and the drops are sheer.

4 2:00: TR at a junction with a signpost (easy to miss) and descend steeply on a rocky path.

5 2:20: TL at a junction onto Path 403: we recommend that you ignore the official AV1 route which heads to the right (see information box). Just afterwards, TR and descend on a track.

F 2:30: Arrive at **Rifugio Dibona (2037m).**

Time	2:30
Distance	6.7
Ascent	98
Descent	813
Max Altitude	2752
Refreshments	Rifugio Dibona
Accommodation	Rifugio Dibona
Path Numbers	401 → 402 → 404 → 403

4A
Continued from Map 3
Stage 4a
Stage 3
Tunnel Route
Forc. Travenanzes
Forc. Lagazuói
Forc. Col dei Bòs
ZIMA DE FOUZÀRGO
COL DEI BÒS
Rif. Lagazuói
Kaiserjäger Steig
Galleria Lagazuói
CENGIA MARTINI
BOSCO
Da Strobel
PIAN DEI MENÌS
Col Gallina
P.so Falzàrego
Fouzargo
Falzarego
Plan de Fauzàre
Al Sasso di Stria
Rif. Bai de Dò
CASONÀTE
L. Limedes
PENES DE FOUZARGO
VAL DE LIMEDES
CRODA NEGRA
Forc. Averau
BOSCH DE CIAMPESTRIN
COL GIALINÈ
PRE DA PONTIN
SOSAS
FEDARE
©Tabacco SRL 2019
0
1km

4A
Official AV1
Stage 4b
Stage 4c
Stage 5a
Stage v5
Passo Giau Shortcut
Continued on Map 5a
TOFANA DE ROZES
3225
Grotta de Tofana
Rif. A. Dibona
CORDES
ALPE SOTECÒRDES
FRÀTA GRANDA
Casón de Rózes
Casón de Landries
BOSCO DE SARESIN
LANDRIES
CINQUE TORRI
Rif. Scoiattoli
Rif. Cinque Torri
PALES DE RUCURTO
CRÉPE DE RONDE
Forc. Nuvolau
NUVOLAU
Rif. Nuvolau
BECO DE RA MA
FORAME
CIÓSTEGO
M.ga Giau
Ru de Fouzargo
MILIERA
MANTÈL
CIAN PÈ
VALON SCURO

4A

Tofana de Rozes with il Castelletto just in front of it

The Official AV1 to Rifugio Scoiattoli

Paths: 412 – 440

On most maps, the AV1 is shown heading W from Waypoint No.5 of Stage 4a. However, we think that this routing is odd: it takes you almost all the way back to Forcella Col dei Bòs. It also bypasses Rifugio Dibona and Rifugio Cinque Torri, finishing instead at Rifugio Scoiattoli. Furthermore, it takes slightly longer than the Stage 4b route. Accordingly, we prefer to describe a more direct route. There is, however, one advantage to using the official AV1 route: a short distance off the path there is a ski-lift to Rifugio Scoiattoli which can be used to avoid the climb on Stage 4b. Directions for the official AV1 are as follows:

TR at the junction at Waypoint No.5 onto Path 412. On arrival at a track, TL onto it. After a while, TL onto a path (Path 412). TL onto the main road. Shortly afterwards, TR and climb on Path 440. Eventually, TL at a junction. Soon follow a track NE to **Rifugio Scoiattoli (2255m)**.

Rifugio Dibona to Rifugio Cinque Torri

4B

The wonderful views from Rifugio Cinque Torri

Descend through forest and then climb to the famous Cinque Torri ('five towers'), a stunning rock formation. During WW1, the Italian army established artillery headquarters near to Cinque Torri because of the excellent views of the Austrian front-line positions to the N (many of which were passed on Stage 4a). To protect against an Austrian counter-attack, the Italians prepared defensive positions at Cinque Torri: many of the trenches and fortifications have been restored as an open-air war museum which is just off the AV1.

Time	1:45
Distance	4.5
Ascent	408
Descent	308
Max Altitude	2137
Refreshments	Rifugio Cinque Torri
Accommodation	Rifugio Cinque Torri
Path Numbers	442 → 439

Rifugio Cinque Torri is situated just below the towers. It serves some of the best food on the AV1. The paths on this stage can be muddy and slippery. Navigation is straightforward.

4B

Approaching the Cinque Torri from the E

S See Map 4A. Descend S on a broad track. After a few minutes, TR onto Path 442 and descend through forest.

1 0:35: Cross the main road and keep SH on a tarmac lane. 5min later, TR and climb on Path 439.

2 1:30: TR onto another path: you should see Cinque Torri up ahead. 10min later, TL up a small road.

F 1:45: Shortly afterwards, arrive at **Rifugio Cinque Torri (2137m)**.

Rifugio Cinque Torri to Rifugio Nuvolau

4C

The climb towards Rifugio Nuvolau

A short climb to two of the most famous rifugi on the AV1: Rifugio Averau with its legendary cooking and Rifugio Nuvolau with its legendary sunset views. The route also passes close to Rifugio Scoiattoli which has a wonderful setting looking over the Cinque Torri and the mountains across the valley to the N.

Navigation is straightforward. There is a broad track all the way to Averau. Then there is a path up to Nuvolau.

You can also access Rifugio Scoiattoli using a ski-lift from the valley floor. This is a good way to get onto the AV1 if joining from Cortina d'Ampezzo: the bus will drop you near the foot of the uplift.

Time	1:15
Distance	2.2
Ascent	438
Descent	0
Max Altitude	2575
Refreshments	Rifugio Scoiattoli Rifugio Averau Rifugio Nuvolau
Accommodation	Rifugio Scoiattoli Rifugio Averau Rifugio Nuvolau
Path Numbers	439

4C

Walking the ridge beside Rifugio Scoiattoli

S See Map 4A. Pick up Path 439 behind the rifugio. Just afterwards, TL on a track.

1 0:15: Arrive at a junction where there are three options: TR if you wish to go to **Rifugio Scoiattoli (2255m)** which is only 5min away; TL for the Passo Giau Short-cut (see information box); or keep SH to continue on Stage 4c. Soon TL at a junction of tracks. Shortly afterwards, TL at another junction, climbing on a track.

2 0:45: Arrive at **Rifugio Averau (2413m)**. Climb SE on Path 439.

F 1:10: Arrive at **Rifugio Nuvolau (2575m)**.

Passo Giau Short-cut

Path 443 travels from Waypoint No.1 directly to Passo Giau. It enables you to avoid the cabled sections on Stage 5a.

1 0:15: See Map 4A. From red Waypoint No.1, head SE on Path 443. 10min later, keep SH at a junction and descend steeply. 10min later, start to climb steeply. The undulating path is slippery after rain.

1 1:10: Keep SH at a junction: here you join Stage 5a of the main AV1.

2 1:35: See Map 5A. TL onto a track. Shortly afterwards, arrive at **Passo Giau (2236m)**.

Rifugio Nuvolau to Passo Giau

5A

Passo Giau: notice the hole in the face of Tofana de Rozes behind. This was caused by the mine in WW1

This is one of the most talked about sections of the AV1. From the rifugio, head across rock: the views are exquisite in all directions. Soon, arrive at the crux of the stage: the two exposed descents with cables bolted into the rock to assist. These sections are probably not as difficult as legend suggests, and most people have no difficulties, but a head for heights is required. As you descend, the rock gives way to grass and you enter some of the finest scenery on the AV1. Passo Giau, with its little chapel, is a beautiful place to stay.

The less-confident may wish to avoid the cabled sections altogether by using the Passo Giau Short-cut (See Stage 4c) which rejoins the main AV1 at Waypoint No.1 of Stage 5a. If using the short-cut, unless you have your heart set on Averau/Nuvolau, it is preferable to stay at Rifugio Cinque Torri or Rifugio Scoiattoli: this avoids having to climb to Averau/Nuvolau and then descend back to Rifugio Scoiattoli the next day to access the short-cut.

Time	1:30
Distance	2.5
Ascent	60
Descent	399
Max Altitude	2575
Refreshments	Berghotel Passo Giau
Accommodation	Berghotel Passo Giau
Path Numbers	438 → 443

Take great care on the cabled sections as a fall would be serious. Avoid this stage in wet conditions when the rocks would be slippery: use the Passo Giau Short-cut instead.

In summer there is a bus between Passo Giau and Cortina d'Ampezzo (Dolomitibus Line 30/4: see www.dolomitibus.it). This can be used to leave or join the AV1.

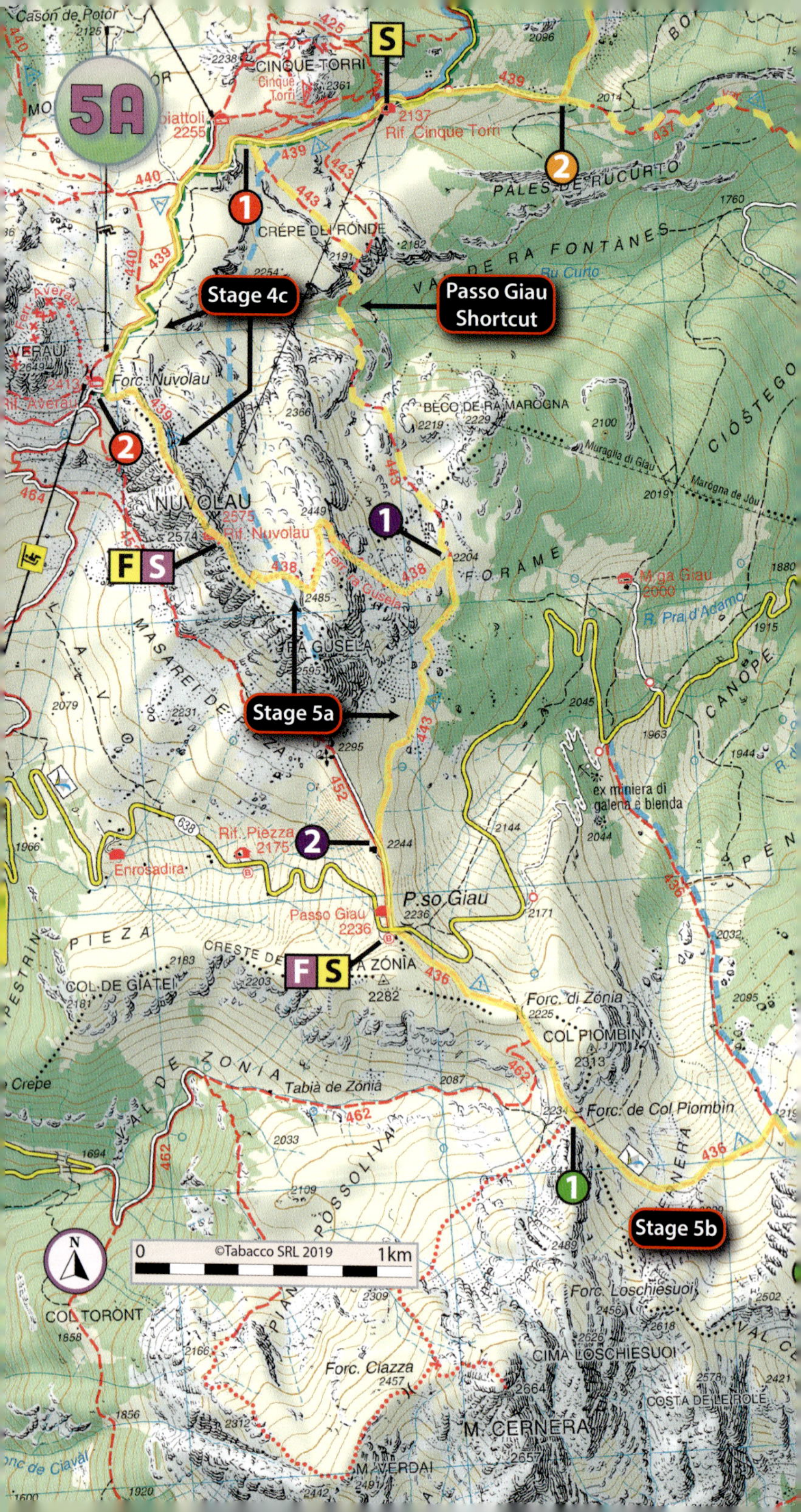
5A
S
Stage 4c
Passo Giau
Shortcut
Stage 5a
Stage 5b
F S
CINQUE TORRI
Rif. Cinque Torri
2137
CRÉPE DE RONDE
PALES DE RUCURTO
VAL DE RA FONTANES
Forc. Nuvolau
Rif. Averau
NUVOLAU
Rif. Nuvolau
BECO DE RA MAROGNA
FORAME
M.ga Giau
RA GUSELA
Ferr. ra Gusela
Rif. Piezza
Enrosadira
P.so Giau
Passo Giau
2236
PIEZA
COL DE GIATEI
CRESTE DE
Forc. di Zónia
COL PIOMBIN
Forc. de Col Piombin
VAL DE ZONIA
Tabià de Zónia
POSSOLIVA
ex miniera di galena e blenda
CANOPE
COL TORONT
Forc. Loschiesuoi
CIMA LOSCHIESUOI
Forc. Clazza
M. CERNERA
M. VERDAI
COSTA DE LE ROLE
©Tabacco SRL 2019
0
1km

Continued from Map 4a
Stage v5
Continued on Map 6a
PERONATE
CRÉPE DE
SCUDELER
BUS DEL TIZON
BÈCO D'AIAL
Bèco d'Aial
P.te de Rucurto
CASON DE FORMIN
CIOU DE RA MAZA
PENES
VAL DE FORMIN
CIADENES
VAL NEGRA
LARZIE
FORZEL
L. Ciou de ra Maza
L. de Federa o da Lago
Rif. Croda da Lago G.Palmieri 2046
C. BASSA DA LAGO
P.TA FRAIO
CRODA DA LAGO
C. AMBRIZZOLA
PONTA DE GIAU
GRAN DIEDRO
Forc. de Formin
Forc. Rossa
PONTA LASTOI DE FORMIN
SPIZ DE MONDEVAL
Forc. Giau
Forc. Ambr
Sepoltura mesolitica
C.n Mondeval de sora
R. d'Ambrizzola
P.te di Sassi
Forc. Col Duro

5A

A view from Passo Giau

5A

Admiring the spectacular views on the climb to Forcella Giau (Stage 5b)

S See Map 5A. Head initially SE on Path 438: follow waymarks closely. Shortly afterwards, descend the first of the cabled sections. Then follow waymarks SE across rock. Ignore a path on the right. Shortly afterwards, bear left heading N. Soon, bear right and enter the second cabled section. Afterwards, continue downhill, following waymarks through rock and grass.

1 1:00: TR at a junction: the Passo Giau Short-cut rejoins the AV1 here.

2 1:25: TL onto a track.

F 1:30: Shortly afterwards, arrive at **Passo Giau (2236m)**.

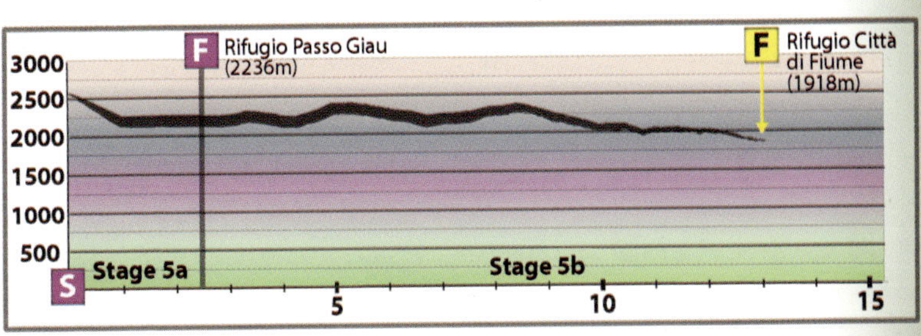

5B

The views back towards Passo Giau from Forcella de Col Piombìn

S See Map 5A. Head SE on Path 436. After 15min, TL at a fork.

1 0:25: TL at **Forcella de Col Piombìn (2234m)**. 15min later, TR at a junction and climb steeply.

2 1:15: Keep SH across **Forcella Giau (2357m)**. Head along a ridge: soon, the path splinters and drops to the left of it into a valley (waymarks on posts).

3 1:45: The path crosses a stream. 15min later, keep SH at a junction.

4 2:15: TR at **Forcella Ambrizzola (2274m)**, still on Path 436: traverse S across limestone slopes.

5 2:35: See Map 6A. At **Forcella Col Duro (2295m)**, bear left and start to descend.

6 3:00: At the farm buildings at **Prendera (2144m)**, TR and descend on a track (Path 458). Stay on this track, ignoring offshoots.

7 3:25: At **Forcella Roan (1999m)**, keep SH climbing briefly (Path 467). Then descend again.

F 4:00: Arrive at **Rifugio Città di Fiume (1918m)**.

Passo Giau to Rifugio Città di Fiume

5B

The unusual angles of the mountains are striking

Leaving Passo Giau, an incredible traverse leads you across grassy slopes decked with wildflowers and surrounded by magnificent peaks. Many passes are crossed on this stage, each of which offers stunning views, but the third one (Forcella Giau) is the highlight: here you enter a Dolomite wonderland of green pastures and limestone where the unusual angles of the mountains are unforgettable. After the fourth pass, Forcella Ambrizzola, traverse a starkly beautiful zone of white limestone and then start the long descent to the popular Rifugio Città di Fiume.

In good conditions, navigation is largely straightforward on the clear paths and tracks. However, take care to follow the waymarks on the short descent after Forcella Giau. Some of the paths are muddy after rain. Do not undertake this stage in bad weather or low visibility as it passes through some exposed and remote terrain.

Time	4:00
Distance	10.6
Ascent	386
Descent	704
Max Altitude	2357
Refreshments	Rifugio Città di Fiume
Accommodation	Rifugio Città di Fiume
Path Numbers	436 → 458 → 467

V5

A misty morning near Forcella Ambrizzola

S See Map 5A. From Rifugio Cinque Torri, head E on the road. After a few minutes, TR onto Path 439. 5min later, TR at a junction (Waypoint No.2 of Stage 4b) onto Path 437. Soon TR at another junction and continue descending.

1 0:45: Cross a road and pick up Path 437 on the other side. Soon start to climb through the forest.

2 1:30: Shortly after crossing a stream, ignore Path 435 on the right. Shortly afterwards, TR at a junction onto Path 434, still climbing. Soon the path bears right and heads S (to the E of the summit ridge of Croda da Lago).

3 2:15: Arrive at **Rifugio Croda da Lago (2046m)**. Pick up Path 434 again at the S end of the lake.

4 3:00: Cross **Forcella Ambrizzola (2274m)** and rejoin the main AV1: TL on Path 436 and traverse S across limestone slopes.

5 3:20: See Map 6A. At **Forcella Col Duro (2295m)**, bear left and start to descend.

6 3:45: At the farm buildings at **Prendera (2144m)**, TR and descend on a track (Path 458). Stay on this track, ignoring offshoots.

7 4:10: At **Forcella Roan (1999m)**, keep SH, climbing briefly (Path 467). Then descend again.

F 4:45: Arrive at **Rifugio Città di Fiume (1918m)**.

Rifugio Cinque Torri to Rifugio Città di Fiume (via Rifugio Croda da Lago)

V5

Stage v5 passes to the E side of the Croda da Lago summit ridge

This variant is not quite as scenic as the main AV1 but it is still lovely. Rifugio Croda da Lago has a magnificent setting beside Lago de Federa and is a fabulous place to stay: because it is tucked away on an AV1 variant, it is often very peaceful, attracting fewer overnight visitors.

At Forcella Ambrizzola (Waypoint No.4), rejoin the main AV1: traverse a starkly beautiful zone of white limestone and then start the long descent to the popular Rifugio Città di Fiume.

In good conditions, navigation is generally straightforward. Some of the paths are muddy after rain. Do not undertake this stage in bad weather or low visibility as it passes through some exposed and remote terrain.

Time	4:45
Distance	13.6
Ascent	645
Descent	864
Max Altitude	2295
Refreshments	Rifugio Croda da Lago; Rifugio Città di Fiume
Accommodation	Rifugio Croda da Lago; Rifugio Città di Fiume
Path Numbers	439 → 437 → 434 → 436 → 458 → 467

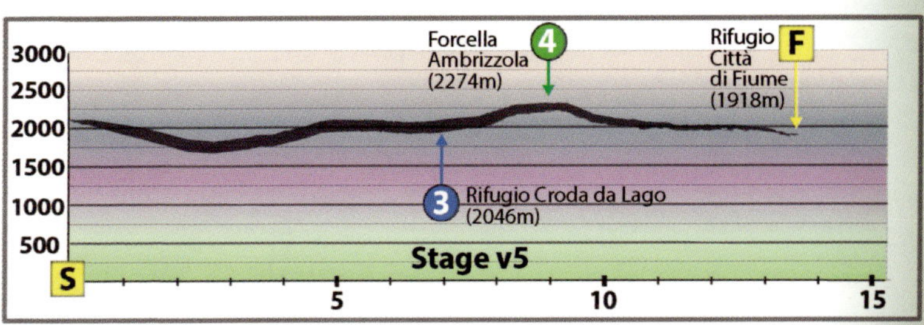

6A
Continued from Map 5a
Stage 5b
Stage 6a
©Tabacco SRL 2019
0
1km
Forc. Ambrizzola
BECO DE MEZODÌ
Forc. de So
Forc. Col Duro
COL DURO
LA ROCHETA DE PRENDERA
ROCHETA DE LA RUOIBES
C.ra Prendera
Forc. de Col Roan
Taulà de la Ruòibes
COL ROAN
LE FOPE
COL DEL TERMINE
Forc. Roan
Forc. de la Puina
MONT DEL FEN
COL FORMOS
LE SALE
COL DE LA PUINA
Ru Anteimon
Ru Avace
VIZA DE BAGN
Forc. Costantìol
Rif. Città di Fiume
M.ga Fiorentina
Rif. Aquileia
Camping Cadore
S.Antonio
Forc. Foràta
T. Fiorentina
Cave di ghiaia
CRODA TORONDA
SALE DE CRODA TORONDA
Dolomiten Höhenweg
M. CROT
Rif. P.so Staulanza
P.so Staulanza
Nevato di Val d'Arcia
PELMO
F
S
1
4
5
6
7

Rifugio Città di Fiume to Rifugio Passo Staulanza

6A

Wide-ranging views from the balcony path below the Pelmo

A short but spectacular stage which traverses the NW slopes of the famous Pelmo (3168m). On Stage 6b, you will get to enjoy the Pelmo from afar but here you pass right next to it: the sheer walls of the mountain are breathtaking. Afterwards, descend through forest to Rifugio Passo Staulanza which is developing a reputation as a more luxurious place to stay. It is more expensive but we think it is worth it. Navigation and terrain are straightforward.

Time	1:00
Distance	3.1
Ascent	56
Descent	208
Max Altitude	1918
Refreshments	Rifugio Passo Staulanza
Accommodation	Rifugio Passo Staulanza
Path Numbers	472

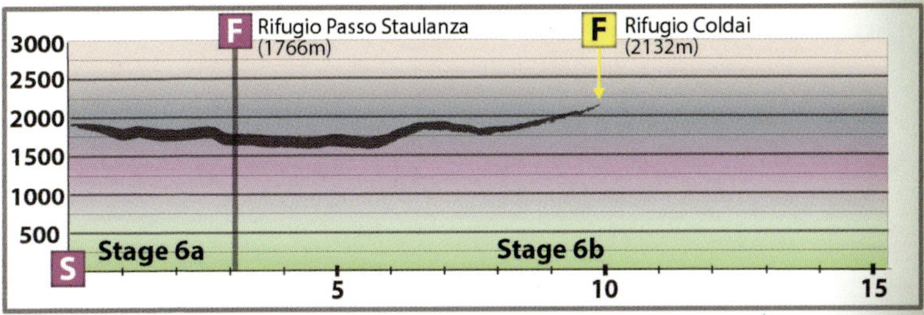

The famous Pelmo (3168m)

S See Map 6A or 6B. Walk 100m back down to the track travelled on Stage 5b: cross over onto Path 472 and descend through forest.

1 0:25: The path crosses a large zone of boulders and shale: watch your footing. Afterwards, descend through trees again.

F 1:00: Arrive at **Rifugio Passo Staulanza (1766m)**.

Rifugio Passo Staulanza to Rifugio Coldai

6B

The sunsets at Rifugio Coldai are legendary

This link route travels between the Pelmo and the Civetta. As you proceed, the views of the Pelmo get better and better, culminating with the incredible viewpoint at Rifugio Coldai. The sunset at the rifugio is legendary: the soft, low light hits the Pelmo's SW face, painting it a glorious shade of orange. The food is excellent and the helpings are enormous.

The section between Casera Vescovà and Casera di Pioda is tricky to navigate as there are no signs or waymarks. The climb above Casera Vescovà is steep and muddy. The final climb to Rifugio Coldai is also steep in places and the path splinters frequently: follow the waymarks carefully.

Time	2:30
Distance	6.8
Ascent	528
Descent	162
Max Altitude	2132
Refreshments	Casera Vescovà Rifugio Coldai
Accommodation	Rifugio Coldai
Path Numbers	568 → 561 → 556

6B
Stage 6a
Stage 6b
Continued on Map 7a
F S
Rif. Città di Fiume
M.ga Fiorentina
Rif. Aquileia
Camping Cadore
B.ta Flora Alpina
M. CROT
COL DI AGUSCIEI
Rif. P.so Staulanza
P.so Staulanza
C.ra Staulanza
Dolomiten Höhenweg
Anello Zoldano
CRODA TORONDA
PIAN DEI BUOI
PALA DE LE DEE
VAL DEI ZIRAI
COL DE LA TRAVERSA
Rif. Pala Favera
Rif. M. Pelmo
Camping Pala Favera
Alta Via Dolomiti
PIAN DE LE MANDRATE
CORNIA
COL DI VALLON
Pecol Vecchio
Pecol Nuovo

6B
Stage v6
Forc. Foràta
S.Antonio
CIMA FORADA
Forc. Val d'Arcia
SAS DE LA GRIES
CRODE DI FORCA ROSSA
Forca Rossa
Nevato di Val d'Arcia
PELMO
PELMETTO
La Fessura
SPALLA EST
SPALLA SUD
PALA SUD
Rif. Venezi A. De Luca
CAMPI DI RUTORTO
P.so di Rutorto
LA DAMBRA
CREPE DE LA VARELLA
VAL D'AGNEL
LE MANDRE
COSTAUTA
SPELZI
CAMPI SO' PELF
Tabià del Fuma
SASS DE FORMEDAL
PIERA DAL BOSCH
Forc. dei Mur
Miniera abbandonata
Baita di Daré Dôf
Ru Sfondra
Ru Torto
©Tabacco SRL 2019
0
1km

6B

Rifugio Coldai at sunrise

S See Map 6B. Walk W down the road on a path just to the left of it (Path 568). Just after leaving the rifugio, Path 472 on the left is confusingly signed as the AV1: ignore this unless you wish to head to Camping Palafavera, Rifugio Palafavera or Rifugio Pelmo (see Stage v6).

1 0:15: At a hairpin bend, keep SH on a track.

2 0:35: See Map 7A. TL at a fork, descending on a tarmac lane. 10min later, TL immediately after the farm buildings of **Casera Vescovà o Bela Mont (1734m)** which serves meals: climb steeply on Path 561. After a while, the path becomes a grassy track.

3 1:15: When you meet a gravel track, keep SH descending gently on it. 5-10min later, TR onto a path (no waymarks) which descends towards a junction where there is a building. TL onto a gravel track. Just afterwards, TR at the junction onto another track ('Rifugio Coldai').

4 1:30: A few minutes later, arrive at **Casera di Pioda (1816m)**: this is where Stage v6 rejoins the main AV1. TR at the building and climb on Path 556: follow waymarks to stay on the main path, ignoring offshoots. The gradient increases higher up. The final approach to the rifugio is sensational.

F 2:30: Arrive at **Rifugio Sonino al Coldai (2132m)**.

Rifugio Città di Fiume to Rifugio Coldai (via Rifugio Venezia)

V6

The view E from Rifugio Coldai

An exceptional variant making a clockwise circumnavigation of the Pelmo: the views are breathtaking, particularly at Forcella Val d'Arcia. Rifugio Venezia, about half-way along the stage, is a spectacular place to stay and the sunsets are magnificent. The second half of the stage is less dramatic but still beautiful. However, the climb up the track from Pala Favera to Casera di Pioda is a little monotonous.

The beauty is not given away cheaply though as the stage is challenging. The tough climb to Forcella Val d'Arcia is very steep and there are long sections of scree. The steep descent from the pass is also difficult: the scree is loose and unstable. Sections of the route are exposed and a head for heights is necessary. There are a few cabled sections too. In short, this is a route for the more experienced walker.

Navigation on both sides of Forcella Val d'Arcia is tricky in places: follow waymarks carefully. Do not undertake this stage in bad weather or low visibility as it passes through some exposed and remote terrain.

In high summer, you can avoid the climb from Pala Favera to Casera di Pioda by using a ski-lift: from the top of the uplift, follow a track W for 10min to reach Casera di Pioda. There is a small grocery shop at the campsite at Pala Favera.

Time	7:30
Distance	16.8
Ascent	1320
Descent	1106
Max Altitude	2476
Refreshments	Rifugio Venezia Pala Favera Rifugio Coldai
Accommodation	Rifugio Venezia Pala Favera Rifugio Coldai
Path Numbers	480 → 471 → 472 → 474 → 564 → 556

A moody day near Casera di Pioda

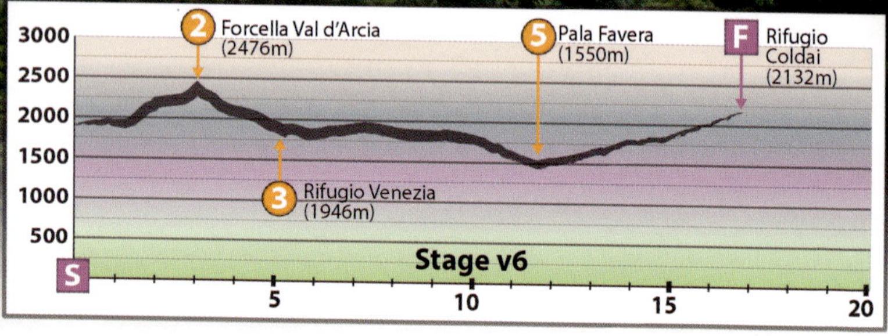

S See Map 6B. Walk 100m back down to the track travelled on Stage 5b: cross over onto Path 480 and climb through trees.

1 TR at **Forcella Foràta (1977m)**, still on Path 480: this path is narrow and sometimes hard to follow. Soon, TL into a gulley and climb steeply (initially SE), following waymarks. After a while there is a cabled section: take care. There are also sections of scree and boulders: follow waymarks carefully.

2 2:40: Keep SH across **Forcella Val d'Arcia (2476m)** and descend a steep scree slope: take care. Soon, there are some exposed sections protected by cables.

3 3:50: Arrive at **Rifugio Venezia A. De Luca (1946m)**. Head S on Path 471. 5-10min later, TR at **Passo di Rutorto (1931m)** onto Path 472.

4 5:00: TL at **Col de le Crepe Cavaliere (1884m)** onto Path 474: if you TR onto Path 472, you can take a short detour to view some dinosaur footprints (follow signs; 15min each way).

5 5:30: TL onto the road at **Pala Favera (1550m)** where there are two rifugi, a campsite and a ski-lift (see above). 5min later, TR onto a track (Path 564) and climb through forest.

6 6:30: See Map 7A. TL just after **Casera di Pioda** and climb on Path 556: you are now back on the main AV1. Follow waymarks to keep on the main path, ignoring offshoots. The gradient increases higher up. The final approach to the rifugio is sensational.

F 7:30: Arrive at **Rifugio Sonino al Coldai (2132m)**.

Rifugio Coldai to Rifugio Tissi

7A

The viewpoint above Rifugio Tissi is one of the finest on the AV1

This stage is another highlight of the AV1. A short climb brings you to Forcella Coldai where you leave the Pelmo behind and catch sight of the incredibly scenic Lago Coldai, resting underneath the immense walls of the Civetta. After passing the lake, an amazing balcony path skirts below the cliffs of the mountain: a humbling experience. Finally, climb to Rifugio Tissi which has sublime views of the Civetta: 5min above the rifugio there is an even better viewpoint with a 360° panorama.

In fact, Rifugio Tissi is just off the official route of the AV1 which keeps SH at Waypoint No.4, taking a more direct route to Rifugio Vazzoler (see Stage 7b). However, the views from Rifugio Tissi are so special that we have decided to include it on our main route: on a fine day, it would be a travesty to miss it.

The path is clear but it is sometimes rocky and unstable. Navigation is straightforward except around Lago Coldai where there is a confusing labyrinth of paths. The stage is well marked.

Time	2:30
Distance	4.7
Ascent	435
Descent	317
Max Altitude	2250
Refreshments	Rifugio Tissi
Accommodation	Rifugio Tissi
Path Numbers	560 → 563

7A
COL DI DAVAGNIN
PIAN DEL CIAVAL
STRENTE
VALDAIER 1634
PISTORNA
PRA DELLA COSTA
La Tiezza
COL DE FRENE
LAVADOI
Fernazza
-di sopra
Pradèl-
R. delle Sorize
Col
Piani di Pezzè
PIAN DI PEZZÈ
B.ta Scoiattolo
Fontanabona
PRA MARCON
FONTANA BONA
Col
Coldemies
Ru dell'Alva
VAL DE MOLIN
I Molini
Fontanive
B.ta da Teno
OTEARA
SORA SASSEL
SASSEL
TAPP DALE PAROLE
CREPE DI FALCONERA
LA TAPPA
LA VELMA
C. OVEST DI COLDAI
VAL D'ANTERSASS
T. Zunaia
Ru de Porta
Ru Antersass
PALA DE LA FOIA
L. Coldai
LA ROCCA
COL NEGRO DI COLDAI
Stage 7a
RIANE BASSE
LE MARIANE ALTE
RONCH BRUSA
Dolomiten Höhenweg
DI VALGRANDE
CAST. DI VALGRANDE
T. DA LAGO
F
S
CIMA DI COL REAN
Rif. A. Tissi
PAN DI ZUCCHERO
PORTA
Continued on Map 7b
P.TA CIVETTA
Via Ferr. degli Alleghesi
Forc. di Col Reàn
P.TA TISSI
CIVETTA
Alta Via Dolomiti
C. DE GASPERI
PICCOLA CIVETTA
Rif. M. V. Torrani
PIAN DELLA TENDA
CIMA SU ALTO
Giazzèr

7A
Stage 6b
Continued from Map 6b
Stage v6
Anello Zoldano
VAL POSEDERA
PALA DA STÓNF
C.ra Vescovà o Bela Mont
COL DEI BALDI
Col dei Baldi
ROA BIANCA
Ru Pala da Stónf
Ru Canedo
Tabià Pioda
COL DI DOF
COL MARIN
COL DE LA TRAVERSA
Forc. di Alleghe
C.ra di Pioda
Rif. Pala Favera
Rif. A. Sonino al Coldai
BUSA DEL TORO
C.ra de Righes
Ru dei Serrai
COL DI VALLE
Pecol Vecchio
LA TIEDA
T. Maè
C.ra del Zorzi
Camping Civetta
CRODOLON
MANDRE DI SOPRA
MASARÉ
SCHENAL DEL BECH
LE FOPE
VAL DI PECOL
B.ta Civetta
CREP DI PECOL
Rif. Pian del Crep
PIAN DE CRISTELIN
LAVINAL GRAND
VALLE CIVETTA
©Tabacco SRL 2019
0
1km

7A

The path climbing to Col Negro di Coldai

7A

Rifugio Tissi has an unique setting, perched high above the valley on an outcrop

S See Map 7A. Take Path 560 which climbs behind the rifugio. Just afterwards, TR at a junction ('Lago Coldai').

1 0:15: Arrive at **Forcella Coldai (2191m)**, a fabulous viewpoint above **Lago Coldai**. There is an array of paths: take the one which heads around the right side of the lake and then bends left, climbing to a little saddle. Afterwards, an undulating path traverses the slopes below the incredible limestone walls of the Civetta.

2 0:50: Cross **Col Negro di Coldai (2203m)**. Shortly afterwards, TR at a junction, descending on an incredible balcony path.

3 1:20: Shortly after the path starts climbing again, keep SH at a junction. Soon the path splinters a few times: keep to the main path, ignoring offshoots.

4 1:50: Arrive at a junction: you could go SH to continue directly to Rifugio Vazzoler via Forcella di Col Reàn (2107m), arriving at Waypoint No.1 of Stage 7b after 5-10min. However, TR instead to climb towards Rifugio Tissi on Path 563.

F 2:30: Arrive at **Rifugio Tissi (2250m)**: the tap water is undrinkable so you will have to buy bottled water.

7B
Continued from Map 7a
Stage 7b
Stage 8a
Continued on Map 8a
F S
Rif. Vazzoler
Cap. Trieste
Forc. di Casamatta
Forc. di Col Mandro
Le Forzelete
Pian di Pelsa
C. Favretti
Col del Camp
C.ra di Pelsa
Col delle Capre
C.ra di Corpassa
Col del Mus
Col Negro di Pelsa
Valle del Foram
Val dei Cantoni
Pian delle Taie
Mussaia
C. de Gasperi
Cima Su Alto
Cima Terranova
Torre Su Alto
Cime dei Monachesi
Punta Walker
Cima Listolade
Cima de Toni
Cima Paolina
Anticima Nord
Cima della Busazza
Castello della Busazza
Forc. Cozzi
T. Trieste
Col Palanzin
Rugarös
Col d'Ors
Torretta dell'Orso
Dolomiten Höhenweg
©Tabacco SRL 2019
0
1km
N

Rifugio Tissi to Rifugio Vazzoler

7B

One of the beautiful pastures on the way to Rifugio Vazzóler

The descent to Rifugio Vazzoler takes you through a glorious world of pastures and pine trees as you head around the striking pale peaks of the Civetta's southern extremity. Rifugio Vazzoler, with its excellent garden of Alpine plants, is a great place for an overnight break.

The paths before Waypoint No.2 can be muddy and slippery. Navigation is straightforward and the stage is well marked.

Time	1:45
Distance	5.9
Ascent	75
Descent	611
Max Altitude	2250
Refreshments	Rifugio Vazzoler
Accommodation	Rifugio Vazzoler
Path Numbers	563 → 560

Approaching Rifugio Vazzoler the limestone is so pale that it is almost blinding in the midday sun

Rifugio Vazzoler is surrounded by some of the palest limestone peaks in the whole range

7B

S See Map 7A. Head downhill on the path climbed on Stage 7a. After 5min, TR at a junction.

1 0:20: Keep SH at a junction on Path 560. 30min later, head through a beautiful pasture. Afterwards, pass through a zone of grass and huge boulders. Soon, the views open up and you descend again.

2 1:15: See Map 7B. TL at a junction and go through a gate: easy to miss. 5min later, TL and descend on a steep track. At any junctions, follow signs for 'Rifugio Vazzoler'. When you emerge from the trees again, the views are staggering.

F 1:45: TR at a fork. Just afterwards, arrive at **Rifugio Vazzoler (1714m)**.

8A
Continued from Map 7b
Stage 8a
3
4
5
F
S
COL PALANZIN
1686
TORRETTA DELL'ORSO
CIMON DEL ZOLDO
Forc. delle Nevere
Forc. delle Masenade
LA CATTEDRALE
PALA DELLE MASENADE
Alta Via Dolomiti
TRIDENTE
PALA DEL CAMP
Forc. del Camp
1933
VALORIET
C.ra del Camp
BUSA DEL CAMP
LE STAMERE
COL DEI PASS
1834
Rif. Bruto Carestiato
Sent. Geologico Agordo
554
552
548
547
553
M.ga Framont
1589
Forc. di Sejere
2003
CORNO
DI FRAMONT
2294
MONT ALT
F.lli Rova
Case Nelle
1376
COL NEGRO
1551
COL MARTINEL
1582
PRA DEVAN
C. Pecole
1308
C. Fesòn
F.lli Collelungo
C. Campòn
1195
T. Binàtega
C.ra Cole
T. Framont
C. Colàz
C. Durando
1163
Prà di Naf
F.lli Caodere
F.lli Dòn
F.lli Càle
F.le Cuie
C.e Dugòn
C. Foch
VAL SALINE
VAL CALEDA
©Tabacco SRL 2019
0
1km
N

8A
Stage 8b
Stage 9
Continued
F
S
P.so Duran
Rif. S. Sebastiano
Rif. C. Tome
1601
SASS DEL DURAM
CRODA SPIZA
COLLE DURAN
CREP DI CASAMATTA
COL D'ORTAT
il Cristo
M.ga Càleda nuova
M.ga Càleda vecchia
Forc. Dagarei
1620
CAZZE ALTE
COL MENADAR
PERA DE CASEN
SASS DE LE MARGHERITE
F.li la Fossa
F.li Planèz
F.li Piarzént
F.li Alghera
F.le Rive
F.le Baudon
F.le Casen
CIMA DEL CASTELLO
F.li Prus
Cesurette
C. Vize
F.le Martesae
I Quattro Tabià
V. DI POLES
Pra di Val
F.li Binatega
C. Vie
Dolomiten Höhenweg
Anello Zoldano
Sent. Angelini
549
524
536
578
547
543
544

The balcony path contours around the slopes just above the tree-line

Rifugio Vazzoler to Rifugio Carestiato

8A

Views to the S near Col d'Ours (1826m)

A sublime journey amongst jagged limestone peaks which are bright white against the backdrop of the deep blue sky. Most of the stage is spent on astonishing balcony paths as you skirt the S flanks of the Moiazza group of mountains.

Time	3:45
Distance	9.3
Ascent	627
Descent	507
Max Altitude	1933
Refreshments	Rifugio Carestiato
Accommodation	Rifugio Carestiato
Path Numbers	555 → 554

The terrain is more challenging than that on some previous stages: the path is often rocky and uneven and there are some quite exposed sections. The route is well marked so navigation is largely straightforward. However, there are some sections where the path disappears over rocks: follow the waymarks closely. The altitude is lower than that on previous stages and it can be very hot in the afternoon.

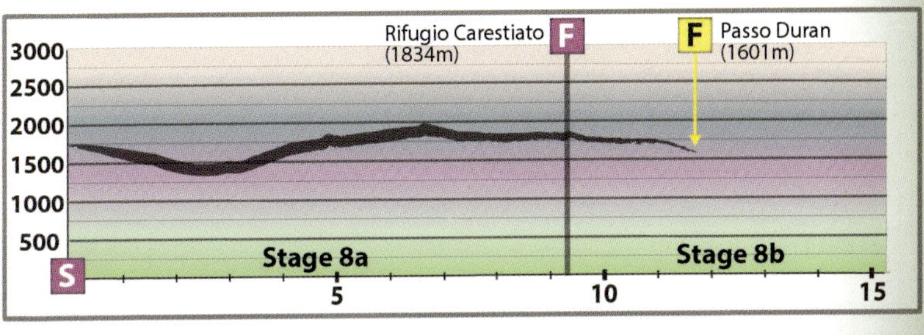

8A

Rifugio Bruto Carestiato

S See Map 7B. Head N to pick up a track (Path 555) which soon descends.

1 0:35: TL onto Path 554 to begin the first climb: alternatively stay on Path 555 for **Rifugio Capanna Trieste (1135m; 2km off-route)**. 20min later, cross a ravine: just afterwards, TL and walk steeply upwards alongside the ravine. Soon the path bears right and shortly afterwards, enters forest again.

2 1:40: Cross a huge ravine littered with boulders and shale: there is no path so follow cairns. Take care as this section is exposed.

3 1:55: Arrive at the narrow **Col d'Ours (1826m)**: to cross it, TL and scramble up a few metres. The narrow path then contours around the slopes: watch your step. There are some cables to assist. Soon cross boulders, following waymarks and cairns.

4 2:40: See Map 8A. At a junction on a grassy plateau, TL and climb steeply: the AV1 route marked on the map differs slightly from the route marked on the ground. 10min later, cross **Forcella del Camp (1933m)** and start to descend.

5 3:00: TL at a fork. Soon, there are sections of boulders where the path largely disappears: follow waymarks and cairns.

F 3:45: Arrive at **Rifugio Bruto Carestiato (1834m)**: the wonderful location more than makes up for the tiny bedrooms.

Rifugio Carestiato to Passo Duran

8B

A morning inversion seen from Rifugio Carestiato

A short stage, descending E to the road-head at Passo Duran. Enjoy far-reaching views to the S. To the E, the peak of Cima Nord di San Sebastiano dominates. There are two rifugi at Passo Duran but no public transport is available. Navigation and terrain are straightforward.

S See Map 8A. Head N on the track to the right of the rifugio. Just afterwards, TR and descend on a path. 5min later, TR onto a track. Just afterwards, TL at a junction on Path 549.

1 0:30: TR onto a path.

F 0:45: A few minutes before arriving at a road, reach a junction: both directions lead to Passo Duran. TR for Rifugio Passo Duran/C.Tomè or TL for Rifugio S. Sebastiano. If you are not stopping at Passo Duran, then it is quicker to TR. A few minutes later, arrive at **Passo Duran (1601m)**.

Time	0:45
Distance	2.4
Ascent	29
Descent	262
Max Altitude	1834
Refreshments	Passo Duran
Accommodation	Passo Duran
Path Numbers	549

8B

Cima Nord di San Sebastiano dominates the views to the E

Passo Duran to Rifugio Pramperet

9

Rifugio Pramperet

After a climb through forest, cross an enormous ravine on a narrow path: the scenery is sublime with the colours of the pale limestone rock, beautiful forest and deep blue skies complimenting each other perfectly. Keep climbing and cross a magnificent pass, Forcella del Moschesin, where there are old military barracks. Take a break here to soak in the views which are some of the finest on the whole trek. An undulating path then makes its way down to a fabulous rifugio with a fabulous setting.

The terrain on this stage is sometimes difficult. The paths amongst the trees are covered with rocks and roots which are slippery after rain. The section across the ravine is rocky and sometimes unstable: the drops are steep so watch your step. Navigation is straightforward.

Time	4:00
Distance	11.4
Ascent	651
Descent	395
Max Altitude	1966
Refreshments	Rifugio Pramperet
Accommodation	Rifugio Pramperet
Path Numbers	543

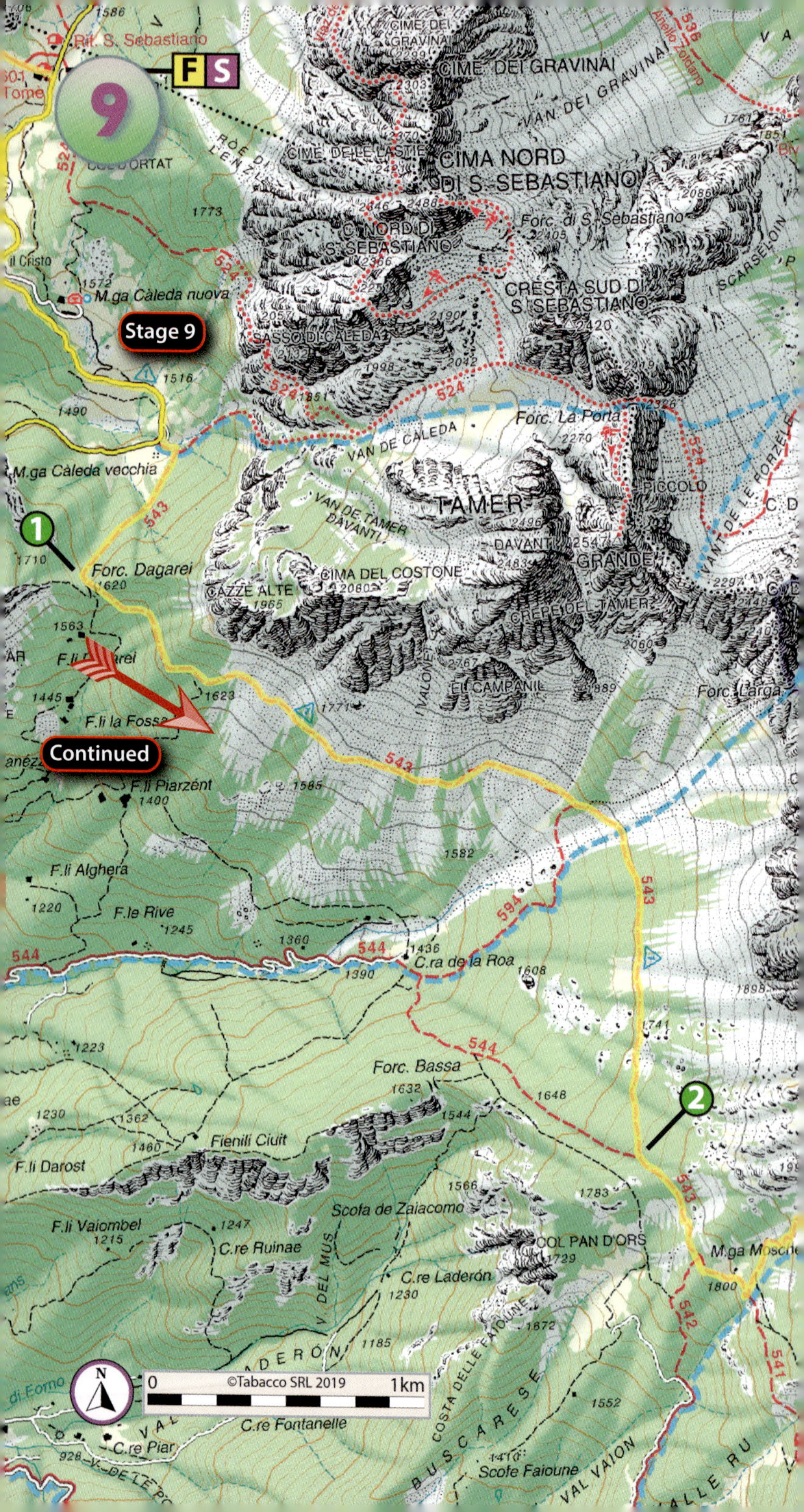
9
F S
Stage 9
Continued
Rif. S. Sebastiano
Col d'Ortat
Cime dei Gravinai
Van dei Gravinai
Cime delle Lastie
Cima Nord di S. Sebastiano
Forc. di S. Sebastiano
C. Nord di S. Sebastiano
Cresta Sud di S. Sebastiano
Sasso di Càleda
M.ga Càleda nuova
M.ga Càleda vecchia
Van de Càleda
Forc. La Porta
Tamer
Van de Tamer Davanti
Piccolo
Davanti
Grande
Cima del Costone
Cazze Alte
Crepe del Tamer
El Campanil
Forc. Larga
Forc. Dagarei
F.li la Fossa
F.li Piarzént
F.li Alghera
F.le Rive
C.ra de la Roa
Forc. Bassa
Fienili Ciuit
F.li Darost
F.li Vaiombel
Scofa de Zaiacomo
C.re Ruinae
C.re Laderón
Col Pan d'Ors
M.ga Moschè
Costa delle Faiolne
Buscarese
Scofe Faioune
Val Vaion
C.re Fontanelle
C.re Piar
0
1km
©Tabacco SRL 2019

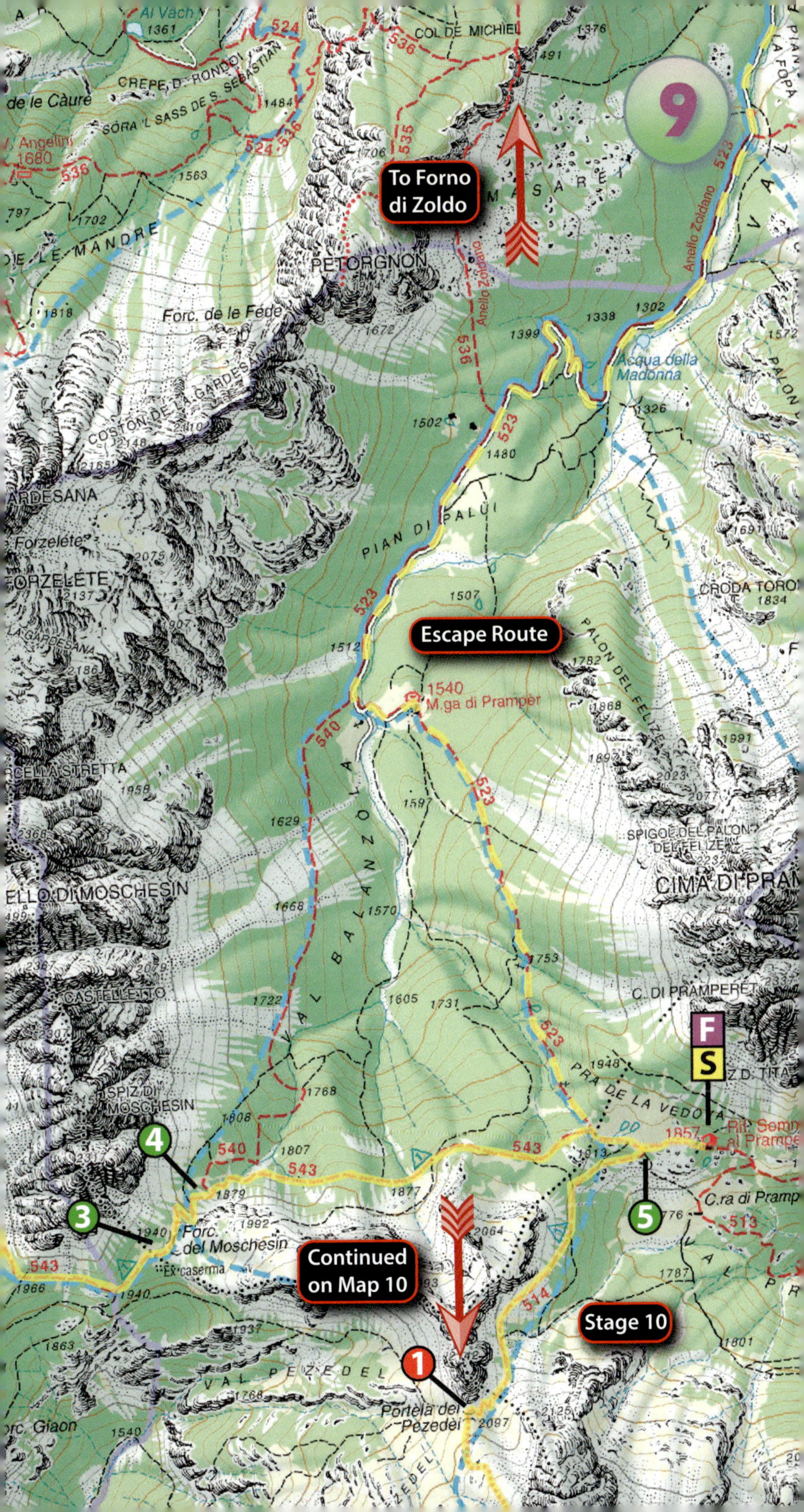

9
To Forno di Zoldo
Escape Route
Continued on Map 10
Stage 10
F
S
COL DE MICHIEL
CREPE D. RONDOI
SORA 'L SASS DE S. SEBASTIAN
PETORGNON
Forc. de le Fede
COSTON DE LA GARDESANA
PIAN DI PALUI
Acqua della Madonna
1540
M.ga di Pramper
PALON DEL FELIZE
CRODA TORO
SPIGOL DEL PALON DEL FELIZE
CIMA DI PRA
C. DI PRAMPERET
PRA DE LA VEDOVA
VAL BALANZOLA
FORZELETE
Forzelete
LA GARDESANA
CASTELLETTO
SPIZ DI MOSCHESIN
Forc. del Moschesin
Ex caserma
VAL PEZEDEL
Portela del Pezedel
C.ra di Pramp
Anello Zoldano

There are many rocky sections on this stage

Walkers approaching Forcella del Moschesin

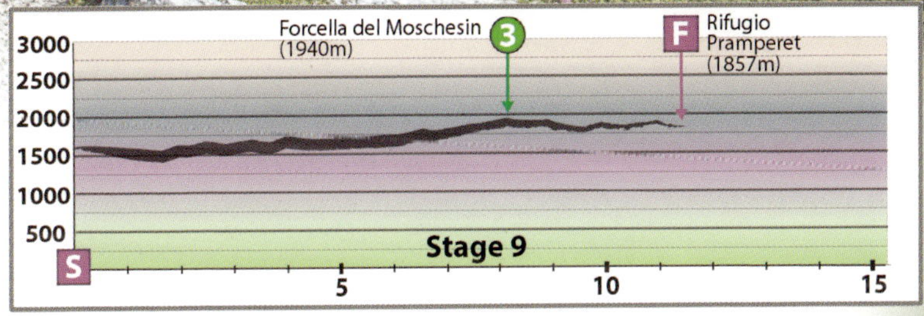

S See Map 8A or 9. Head S down the road. 25min later, TL and climb on Path 543 through forest.

1 0:45: TL at a junction at **Forcella Dagarei (1620m)** and start to descend. 5-10min later, climb again. Soon, emerge from the trees and head towards a ravine. The narrow path traverses the steep slope of the ravine. After the ravine, enter trees again: the going is hard amongst roots and rocks.

2 2:15: TL at a junction and climb. 10min later, pass some buildings in a clearing at **Malga Moschesin (1800m)**: a good place for a break. Pick up the path again just above the buildings. A few minutes later, TL at a junction.

3 3:05: Pass the ruins of old military barracks. Shortly afterwards, cross **Forcella del Moschesin (1940m)**.

4 3:20: TR at a fork (easy to miss): the path on the left (Path 540) would take you directly to Malga di Pramper (see Stage 10). Shortly afterwards, climb steeply up a shale bank. Then, the path undulates.

5 3:55: TL at a junction.

F 4:00: 5min later, arrive at **Rifugio Sommariva al Pramperet (1857m)**.

10
Continued from Map 9
©Tabacco SRL 2019
0
1km
Stage 10
Stage 11a
Stage 11b
Continued on Map 11b
F
S
C.ra di Pramperet
El Pissandol
VAL PRAMPER
COL DE I MUS
Portela del Col de i Mus
COL DE LE
VANT DE LE SCANDOLE DE LA NEF
VAN DE LE SCANDOLE
Portela dei Pezedei
Forc. de Zita nord
Forc. Granda
Forc. de i Scalet
Forc. de Zita sud
CIME DE ZITA
MEZZO
NORD
SUD
LE PRESON
VAN DE ZITADE ENTRO
VAN DE ZITA DE FORA
Forc. dei Erbandoi
TALVENA
CIMA DE LA GIAZA
Forc. de la Giaza
BOSSE DEL VESCOVA
LE STANGHE
Rif. Pian de Fontana
Biv. Dal Mas
Ric. C.ra La Varéta
Forc. La Varéta
V. DE LA SCALA
COL DEI GAI
Dolomiten Höhenweg
Alta Via Dolomiti
VAL DEL BOSCON
MANDRON
SCALON
Alta Via dei Bellunesi
C.ra della Valle
Casonet de Nerville
Rif. F. Bianchet
Variante
PIAN DE LA STUA
513
514
518
520
536
503
537
1245
1632
1709

Rifugio Pramperet to Rifugio Pian de Fontana

10

Views on the final descent to the rifugio

This is the wildest stage of the main AV1 with some of the finest mountain scenery in Europe. For many, it will be the highlight of the whole trek. However, these delights are hard-earned: the climb starts straight out of the blocks and is very steep. The crux of the stage is an exhilarating climb up a knife-edge ridge, leading to a magnificent mountain pass: there the views will take your breath away and all the effort will be forgotten. Afterwards, the first part of the descent to the rifugio is an exceptionally scenic wander through an exquisite grassy valley filled with wildflowers. The second part of the descent is very steep and requires concentration.

Look out for chamois throughout the stage: it pays to get up early as often the first party on the trail sees the most animals.

Do not attempt this stage in bad weather or low visibility. On the climb, the path crosses sections of shale which can be unstable: watch your step. After Portèla dei Pezedèi, take care to follow cairns and waymarks. The final climb up the knife-edge ridge is steep and exposed: there is one short section where you will need to use your hands to scramble upwards. This is the hardest section on the main AV1 and a fall there would be serious so take great care. Many find it thrilling but it requires a head for heights. If you are concerned, you can avoid the stage by taking the escape route to Forno di Zoldo (see Information box): if you exit here then you cannot easily get back onto the AV1 so your trek is over.

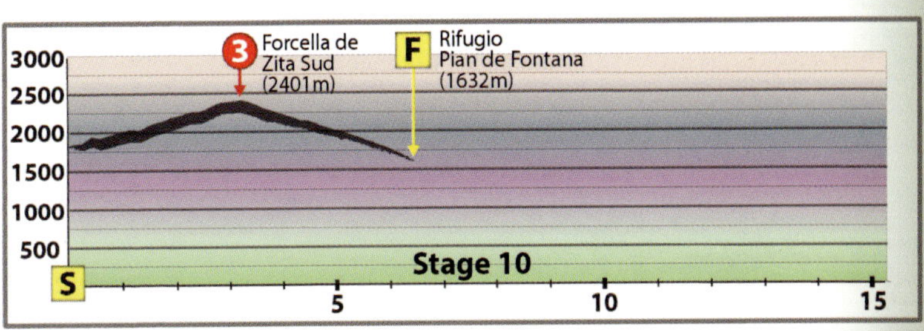

10

After Portèla dei Pezedèi, climb across sections of shale

Time	3:15
Distance	6.4
Ascent	550
Descent	775
Max Altitude	2451
Refreshments	Rifugio Pian de Fontana
Accommodation	Rifugio Pian de Fontana
Path Numbers	514

S See Map 9. Head W back to the junction passed on the previous stage: keep SH and climb on Path 514.

1 0:45: TL at a little saddle, **Portèla dei Pezedèi (2097m)** and continue climbing. Follow cairns when the path disappears over limestone slabs. The views are astonishing. Soon, the path turns to shale and becomes very steep. After a while, keep SH across a grassy plateau. Afterwards, a rocky path climbs steeply.

2 1:35: See Map 10. Arrive on a knife-edge ridge: TL and scramble up steep rocks towards a cairn. Take great care as the drops are sheer. Shortly, reach a small grassy plateau: keep SH up the ridge, following cairns.

3 1:50: Keep SH across **Forcella de Zita Sud (2401m)** and descend. If the path is unclear, follow cairns. Soon, the path bends right and snakes generally SE down a beautiful, grassy valley.

4 2:45: The path dips slightly and then rises gently to a little saddle. Afterwards, continue downhill steeply, sometimes over rocks: watch your footing. There are cable handrails in places.

F 3:15: Arrive at **Rifugio Pian de Fontana (1632m)**.

This knife-edge ridge is arguably the most difficult section of the AV1

Escape Route to avoid Stage 10 (2.75hr)

To exit the AV1, you can walk from Rifugio Pramperet to Malga di Pramper, Pian de la Fopa or Forno di Zoldo. There is a shuttle bus to Forno di Zoldo from Malga di Pramper or Pian de la Fopa: it is available at weekends in June, July and September. In August, it runs every day. Information is available at www.zoldobus.it or +39 348 6700786. From Forno di Zoldo, there is a bus service (Line 25) to Longarone (where there is a train station) and Belluno: www.dolomitibus.it.

See Map 9. From Rifugio Pramperet, retrace your steps W along Path 543. Ignore Path 514 on the left. Shortly afterwards, TR onto Path 523.

0:40: Arrive at **Malga di Pramper (1540m)** which has meals and accommodation (+39 329 7862899; malga.pramper@gmail.com). From there, continue on Path 523 which is now a track: later, TL onto Path 536 only if you wish to head to Camping Al Pez.

1:40: Pass the car park at **Pian de la Fopa**.

2:45: Arrive at **Forno di Zoldo (840m)**.

10

Climbing to Portèla dei Pezedèi with Cima di Pramper in the background

Rifugio Pian de Fontana to Rifugio Bianchet

11A

Sunrise at Rifugio Pian de Fontana

The AV1 is drawing to a close and this stage provides the last great views. A short descent and then a short climb bring you to Forcella la Varéta. Afterwards, a heavenly traverse around the grassy slopes offers wonderful views into Val Vescovà to the W: this is where you are heading. Drop into the valley to the comfortable Rifugio Bianchet.

Navigation and terrain are straightforward.

Time	2:00
Distance	5.8
Ascent	255
Descent	642
Max Altitude	1740
Refreshments	Rifugio Bianchet
Accommodation	Rifugio Bianchet
Path Numbers	514 → 518

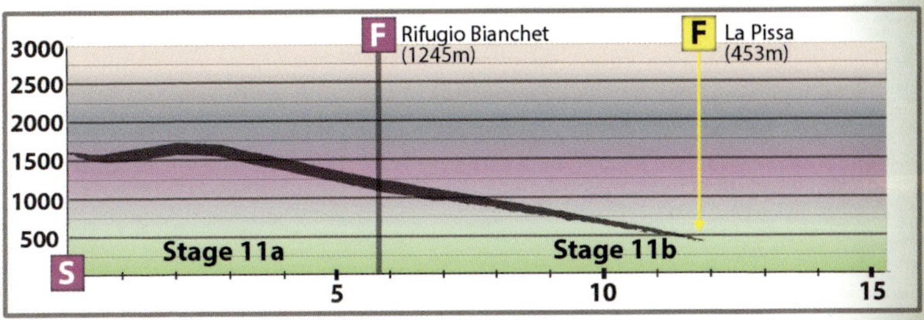

11A

Rifugio Pian de Fontana has an idyllic setting

S See Map 10. From the front of the rifugio, descend across the slopes on Path 514. Soon enter forest.

1 0:15: Just after crossing a stream, TR and climb.

2 0:35: TL at a grassy saddle, **Forcella la Varéta (1704m)**. Soon the narrow path contours around the slopes: take care as the drops are steep.

3 1:05: At approximately 1660m, there is a junction immediately after a huge boulder with faint directions written on it: TL onto Path 514 for Stage v11. Alternatively, keep SH on the main path to continue on Stage 11a (Path 518): descend into the valley.

F 2:00: Arrive at **Rifugio Bianchet (1245m)**.

Sheep grazing near Rifugio Pian de Fontana

The ridge walked on Stage 11a: notice Forcella del Marmol (2262m), which is crossed on Stage v11, above the ridge

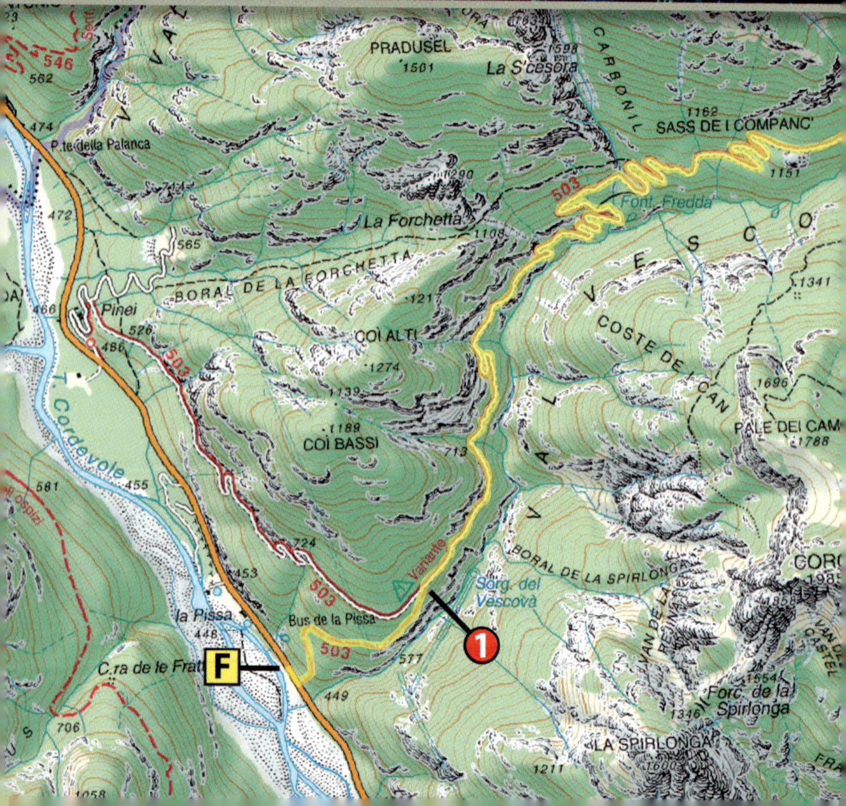

Rifugio Bianchet to la Pissa

11B

11B

A beautiful and easy descent to conclude the AV1. Although you head through forest, there are still some lovely mountain views. The path brings you to the road near la Pissa where you can catch a bus to Belluno (Dolomitibus Line 1). You can buy bus tickets on-board. For timetables, see www.dolomitibus.it.

Time	1:45
Distance	6.1
Ascent	0
Descent	792
Max Altitude	1245
Refreshments	None
Accommodation	None
Path Numbers	503

S See Map 11B. Head W down a track (Path 503): ignore offshoots.

1 1:30: TL onto a path.

F 1:40: TR on a road. Shortly afterwards, cross the road to arrive at the bus stop at **la Pissa (453m)**. Congratulations! You have completed the AV1.

There are plenty of fabulous views between the trees

Rifugio Pian de Fontana to Bolzano Bellunese (Via Ferrata)

V11

Bivacco del Marmol is an unmanned cabin with 9 beds

This variant is by far the most difficult part of the AV1 but it makes for an awesome climax to the trek. A long, tough climb through wild and remote terrain (where there are many chamois) brings you to the sublime Forcella del Marmol. Here the real fun begins because this is the start of a two hour via ferrata (see page 47): an exposed route through beautiful mountain terrain, assisted by metal ladders and cables bolted into the rock-face.

Afterwards, take a break at the lovely Rifugio 7° Alpini which is a wonderful place to spend your final night. A long descent then leads to Bolzano Bellunese where you can catch the bus to Belluno for a celebratory drink.

This stage is very challenging with a lot of climbing and descent. Via ferrata is a dangerous activity and a fall could be fatal. Accordingly, this route should only be undertaken by those with relevant experience who are carrying the correct equipment. Advice on how to undertake a via ferrata is beyond the scope of this book.

Much of the route crosses steep and exposed terrain. Even the sections of the via ferrata which have no cables are extremely steep and exposed. Some scrambling is required. Do not attempt this route in bad weather or low visibility when navigation would be difficult and the terrain would be dangerous. Furthermore, do not attempt the via ferrata if the ground is wet or if rain is forecast: the rocks would be treacherous.

On the climb to Forcella del Marmol, the path is faint and tricky to follow. Often it disappears over scree or limestone slabs: look out for cairns and waymarks (some of which are faded).

From Bolzano Bellunese, you can catch the bus to Belluno (Line L). Check the times in advance at www.dolomitibus.it.

V11
Continued from Map 10
Stage 11a
Stage v11
Continued on next map
LA SCHIARA
BUREL
C.ra della Valle
Casonet de Nerville
Forc. Nerville
COSTA ORTIGA
Forc. del Marmol
Biv. del Marmol
SPALLONE NORD
Ferr. A. Berti
Forc. del Balcon
Biv. U. Dalla Bernardina
Ferr. Zacchi
Rif. 7° Alpini
Forc. Sperti
PALA BERNARDA
TIRON DE MONPIANA
Forc. Monpiana
©Tabacco SRL 2019
0
1km

V11

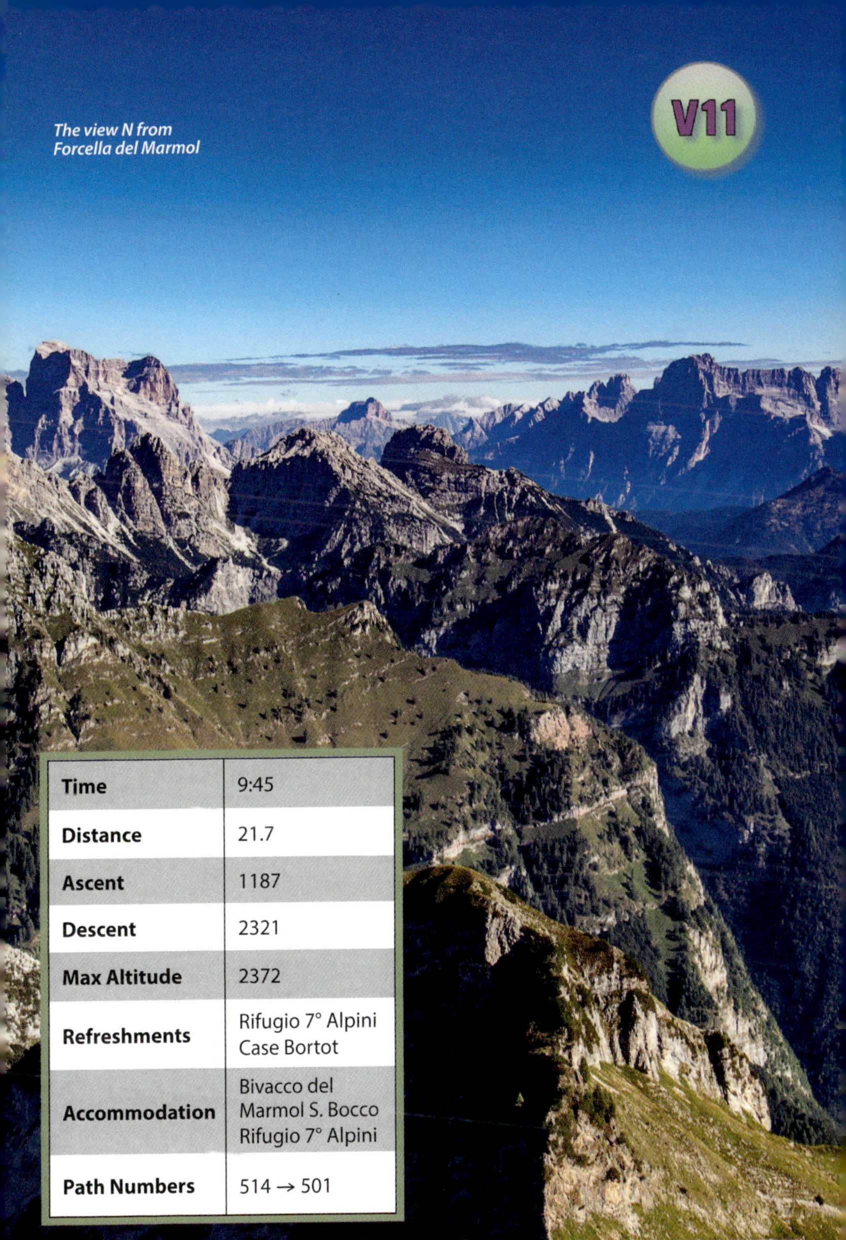

The view N from Forcella del Marmol

Time	9:45
Distance	21.7
Ascent	1187
Descent	2321
Max Altitude	2372
Refreshments	Rifugio 7° Alpini Case Bortot
Accommodation	Bivacco del Marmol S. Bocco Rifugio 7° Alpini
Path Numbers	514 → 501

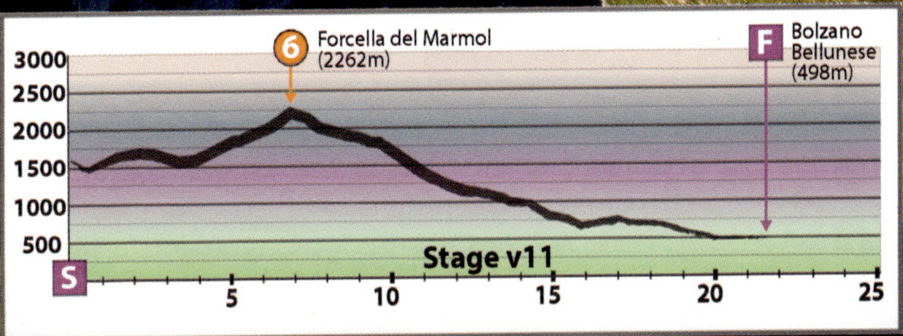

Rifugio 7° Alpini is a great place to spend your final night

See Map 10. Follow the directions for Stage 11a.

3 1:05: See Map V11. At Waypoint No.3 (1660m), TL onto the narrow and overgrown Path 514. 5-10min later, TL immediately after some old buildings and climb steeply on a faint path.

4 2:05: keep SH at a junction on a very faint path (waymarks). A few minutes later, cross a short section of scree and continue upwards on the path on the other side.

5 2:15: The path heads up a grassy spur to the right of a huge rocky gully: follow cairns and/or waymarks when the path disappears amongst scree or rock slabs. The climb is steep and some scrambling is required.

6 3:25: TR at **Forcella del Marmol (2262m)** and continue climbing. Shortly afterwards, bear right across a rock slab, following red arrows. Just afterwards, cairns and waymarks guide you to the start of Via Ferrata Marmol. Put on your via ferrata equipment, clip into the cables and start climbing. 20min later, keep SH at a junction.

7 4:10: Pass **Bivacco del Marmol S. Bocco (2266m)**, a little unmanned cabin with 9 beds. Continue downhill, following waymarks. Now the sections of cabled via ferrata are interspersed with sections unprotected by cables. Navigation is tricky so follow the waymarks carefully.

8 5:10: Keep SH at a junction, descending steeply. 20min later, reach the end of the via ferrata and descend steeply on a narrow path.

9 6:30: Arrive at **Rifugio 7° Alpini (1502m)**: now descend on Path 501.

10 7:55: TR at a junction. A few minutes later, keep SH at another junction, crossing a bridge. The path now climbs for a while and then undulates.

11 8:45: Keep SH through a car park and arrive at the hamlet of **Case Bortot (694m)**. Keep SH past a restaurant, heading down the road.

F 9:45: Arrive in **Bolzano Bellunese (498m)** where you can catch the bus to Belluno.

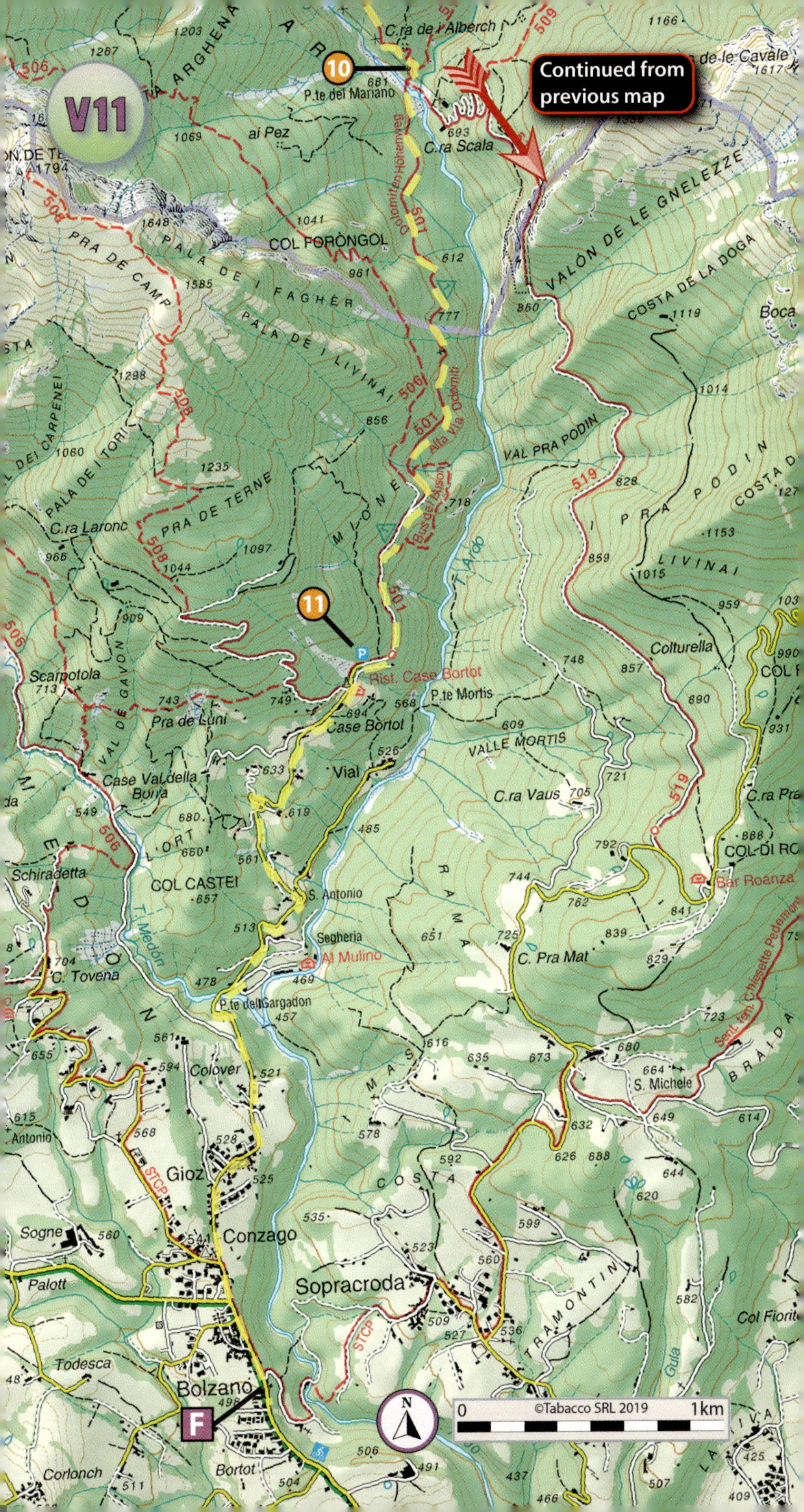
V11
Continued from previous map
C.ra de i Alberch
P.te dei Mariano
C.ra Scala
ai Pez
COL PORÒNGOL
PRA DE CAMP
PALA DE I FAGHÈR
PALA DE I LIVINAI
VALÓN DE LE GNELEZZE
COSTA DE LA DOGA
Boca
Dolomiten Höhenweg
Alta Via Dolomiti
Bus del Tason
VAL PRA PODIN
PALA DE I TORI
C.ra Laronc
PRA DE TERNE
MIONE
T. Ardo
Colturella
Rist. Case Bortot
P.te Mortis
Case Bortot
VALLE MORTIS
Scarpotola
Pra de Luni
VAL DE GAVON
Case Val della Borra
Vial
C.ra Vaus
C.ra Pra
COL DI RO
Bar Roanza
Schiradetta
COL CASTEI
S. Antonio
Segheria
Al Mulino
C. Pra Mat
T. Medòn
C. Tovena
P.te del Gargadon
Colover
S. Michele
BRAIDA
Sent. ten. Chiasette Pedemont
Gioz
Conzago
Sogne
Palott
Sopracroda
COSTA
TRAMONTIN
Col Fiorit
Todesca
Bolzano
F
Bortot
Corlonch
STCP
©Tabacco SRL 2019
0
1km
N

PYGMY ELEPHANT
MM
XV
Journeys worth taking
WWW.PYGMY-ELEPHANT.COM
Tried, tested and trusted self-guided hiking experts since 2016. We make sure that your precious vacation time is planned to perfection.
Simplify the complicated task of planning the Dolomites AV1.
Secure the best accommodation along the trail.
Save time and gain peace of mind with our 24/7 customer service, customizable itineraries and price transparency guarantee.
Book your self-guided tour on the Dolomites AV1 with us today at www.pygmy-elephant.com or use the QR Code below.